SAINTS of A·F·R·I·C·A

SAINTS of A·F·R·I·C·A

VINCENT J. O'MALLEY C.M.

Our Sunday Visitor Publishing Division
Our Sunday Visitor, Inc.
Huntington, Indiana 46750

Our Sunday Visitor Publishing Division
Our Sunday Visitor, Inc.
200 Noll Plaza
Huntington, IN 46750

ISBN: 0-87973-373-X
LCCCN: 2001-131192

Cover design and maps by Monica Haneline

Cover photo, icon of St. Moses the Black, courtesy of
Christ of the Hills Monastery, Blanco, Texas

Interior design by Sherri L. Hoffman

PRINTED IN THE UNITED STATES OF AMERICA

This book is dedicated to
my confreres in the Congregation of the Mission,
known popularly as the Vincentians,
in gratitude for the
education,
formation,
and
inspiration,
which they have given me
for forty years.

CONTENTS

ACKNOWLEDGMENTS

The following persons have assisted me in gathering data for this text: Robert P. Maloney, C.M., and Elmer Bauer, C.M., at the Vincentian Curia at Rome; Joseph P. McClain, C.M., at Mary Immaculate Seminary at Plainsboro, New Jersey; and librarians David Schoen and Samantha Gust, at Niagara University, New York.

Mrs. Myriam Long Witkowski translated from the Italian numerous biographies selected from the *Bibliotheca Sanctorum*.

Critical readers for this text were Linus L. Ormsby, Jr., and Francis X. Prior, C.M., at Niagara University; Michael Ngoka, C.M., of Ankpa, Nigeria; and Thomas O'Hern, C.M., at Nairobi, Kenya.

My secretary, Maria Hamilton, was of inestimable assistance in technological aspects of producing the text.

I thank my family, friends, and professional colleagues for their encouragement and interest during the preparation of this text. I thank especially my uncle, Bartholomew J. O'Malley, C.M.

And I thank two former professors of history, Richard J. Kehoe, C.M., and John W. Carven, C.M., for developing within me a love for reading, researching, and writing history.

INTRODUCTION

Saints of Africa number in the thousands. They include three popes, three Doctors of the Church, eight Fathers of the Church, thousands of martyrs, hundreds of monks, plus countless religious and lay leaders. Africa possesses a rich heritage in the annals of Christian heroes and heroines whom the Church selects as saints. Yet, who among readers in the Western Hemisphere can name more than a few of these saints?

Between the second and sixth centuries, African saints suffered martyrdom under the Roman emperors and Vandal kings. Other African saints left the cities to live in the deserts in a spiritual martyrdom of extraordinary asceticism. Other heroes and heroines remained in the city centers where they fought intellectually for the faith or served practically on behalf of the suffering poor. After Christianity arrived in sub-Saharan Africa in the late fifteenth century, additional saints spent their lives in defense of the religion or in service of the faithful.

The purpose of this book is to highlight some representatives of the literally countless thousands of saints of Africa. In today's global village, it is good for all world citizens to know and appreciate with pride the heritage of sanctity provided by our sisters and brothers in the world's second largest and second most populous continent.

The saints included in this text represent: (1) a variety of geographical places, for example, the Roman provinces in northern Africa and various countries in sub-Saharan Africa; (2) a long span of centuries, for example, the early centuries under the Romans, the Vandal-dominated fifth century, the Renaissance Church in sub-Saharan Africa, the modern Church of the nineteenth and twentieth centuries, and the post-Vatican II contemporary Church; (3) a variety of spiritual experiences, namely martyrdom, monasticism, vowed religious apostolic service, and lay service; (4) both genders, and (5) the gamut of visions, values, and variety of responses to contemporary challenges. These representative saints offer a cross-section of Africa's catalogue of saints. Not included in this book are dozens of saints of non-African origin who ministered in Africa. The scope of this book is saints of the Roman Catholic Church who were either of African origin or of African descent.

As in my previous books, *Saintly Companions* (Alba House, 1995) and *Ordinary Suffering of Extraordinary Saints* (Our Sunday Visitor, 2000), historical accuracy is of paramount importance. In the few instances when data of a doubtful nature are included about the saints, I endeavor to identify clearly those areas about which scholars are still in dispute. The sources most often cited for this study include both scholarly and popular texts, namely the Bollandists' *Acta Sanctorum*, the *Bibliotheca Sanctorum*, Thurston and Attwater's *Butler's Lives of the Saints*, John J. Delaney's *Dictionary of Saints*, the Benedictine monks of Ramsgate Abbey's *The Book of Saints*, and the Bunson family's *Encyclopedia of Saints*, which was published by Our Sunday Visitor in 1998. Primary works of the saints were used as well.

CALENDAR OF FEAST DAYS

January

1   St. Fulgentius
2   St. Macarius the Younger
9   St. Adrian of Canterbury
12 St. Arcadius
15 St. Macarius the Elder
15 St. Isidore of Alexandria
15 St. Paul the Hermit
17 St. Antony of the Desert
20 Bl. Cyprian Michael Iwene Tansi

February

4   St. Isidore of Pelusium
8   St. Josephine Bakhita
9   St. Apollonia of Alexandria and Companions
11 Sts. Saturninus, Dativus, Victoria, and Companions
26 St. Alexander of Alexandria
28 Martyrs of the Alexandrian Plague

March

7   Sts. Perpetua, Felicity, and Companions
12 St. Maximilian
22 St. Deogratias
27 St. John of Egypt
29 Sts. Armogastes and Saturus

April

2   St. Mary of Egypt
4   St. Benedict the Moor
6   St. Marcellinus of Carthage
12 St. Zeno of Verona
20 Sts. Marcellinus, Vincent, and Domninus
27 St. Theodore the Sanctified
30 Sts. Marianus, James, and Companions

May

2   St. Athanasius
3   Sts. Timothy and Maura
9   St. Pachomius
15   St. Isidore of Chios
22   St. Julia of Carthage and Corsica

June

3   St. Charles Lwanga and Companions
3   St. Caecilius
4   St. Optatus
12   St. Onuphrius
15   St. Orsiesius
17   St. Bessarion
27   St. Cyril of Alexandria
30   Ven. Pierre Toussaint

July

1   St. Shenute
3   St. Anatolius
7   St. Pantaenus
13   St. Eugenius
17   St. Speratus and Companions
18   St. Pambo
20   St. Aurelius
28   St. Victor

August

15   St. Alipius
15   Bl. Isidore Bakanja
21   Bl. Victoria Rasomanarivo
24   Martyrs of Utica
27   St. Monica
27   St. Poemen
28   St. Augustine
28   St. Moses the Black
30   Bl. Ghebre Michael

September

6   St. Donatian and Companions
10   St. Nemesian and Companions
11   St. Paphnutius
16   St. Cyprian of Carthage
22   St. Maurice and the Theban Legion

October

1   Sts. Aizan and Sazan
4   St. Ammon the Abbot
8   St. Thais
9   Sts. Athanasia and Andronicus
9   St. Demetrius of Alexandria
10   St. Cerbonius
11   St. Sarmata
12   Sts. Felix of Abbir, Cyprian of Unizibir, and Companions
24   Sts. Aretas and Elesbaan
24   St. Felix of Thibiuca
30   St. Marcellus

November

3   St. Martin de Porres
4   St. Pierius
7   St. Achillas
17   St. Dionysius of Alexandria
21   St. Gelasius
25   St. Catherine of Alexandria
26   St. Peter of Alexandria

December

1   Bl. Anuarite Maria Clementine Nengapeta
3   St. Cassian of Tangier
5   St. Clement of Alexandria
5   St. Crispina
6   Sts. Dionysia, Majoricus, and Companions
10   St. Melchiades
20   St. Ammon the Martyr and Companions

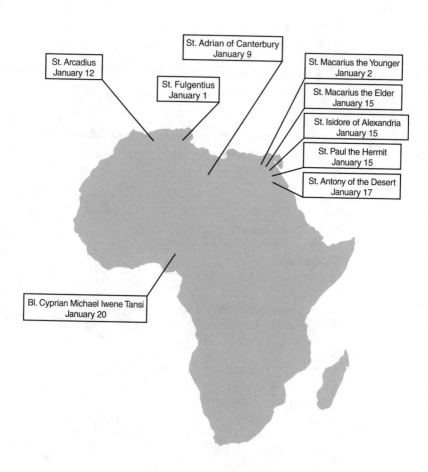

St. Arcadius
January 12

St. Fulgentius
January 1

St. Adrian of Canterbury
January 9

St. Macarius the Younger
January 2

St. Macarius the Elder
January 15

St. Isidore of Alexandria
January 15

St. Paul the Hermit
January 15

St. Antony of the Desert
January 17

Bl. Cyprian Michael Iwene Tansi
January 20

JANUARY

1 ✢ St. Fulgentius

Place: Ruspe, Byzacena (now in Tunisia)
Fame: Monk and bishop, renowned for gentleness

Son of a provincial senator, Fulgentius (468-533) received an excellent classical education, oversaw the family estates on behalf of his widowed mother, and served as lieutenant governor before forsaking power, prestige, and wealth to dedicate his life to God through simple living and truth seeking.

Even as a young man, Fulgentius had earned a reputation for gentleness and solicitousness. "His prudence, his virtuous conduct, his mild carriage to all, and more especially his deference to his mother caused him to be respected wherever his name was known."[1] Although successful and comfortable in the eyes of the world, he frequently visited monasteries in search of a deeper meaning in life. After reading Augustine's commentary on Psalm 36, which contrasts God's goodness and human wickedness, the young man decided to enter the monastic life.

At twenty-two, Fulgentius left Carthage in the province of Africa and traveled a hundred miles south to the remote province of Byzacena, where the exiled bishop Faustus had founded a monastery. Faustus did not grant immediate admission to Fulgentius. The old ascetic asked if the young nobleman, who was so accustomed to the comforts of the wealthy life, would be able to adjust to the austerities of the monastic life. Fulgentius replied affirmatively, declaring that God, who had inspired him, would strengthen him. The elder accepted the younger man's response and invited the aspirant into the community. Shortly thereafter, however, Fulgentius' mother arrived at the front door of the monastery. She had been searching for her missing son. Anxiously, she shouted as she knocked, "Faustus! Restore to me my son and to the people their governor. The Church protects widows; why then, rob you me, a desolate widow, of my son?"[2] All three protagonists sat down and discussed their desires. Ultimately, Fulgentius remained resolutely at the monastery.

An Arian anti-Catholic persecution soon erupted. Faustus and Fulgentius fled for their lives. Fulgentius took refuge in another monastery. After a short time there, the abbot Felix appointed Fulgentius co-abbot; Felix handled the temporal matters and Fulgentius oversaw the spiritual matters. After six years of shared leadership, in 499, another wave of Arian anti-Catholic persecution broke out, causing Fulgentius and Felix to flee. The two monks thought they had found safety at the monastery at Sicca Veneria, until an Arian priest there charged the two refugees with having promoted false teachings. The two were arrested and tortured. Refusing to abandon their faith, they were released with a warning not to continue their ministry.

Fulgentius traveled toward Egypt, where he hoped to meet with and learn from the desert monks there. In Sicily, however, he learned that the Church in Egypt, particularly in the isolated desert colonies, was suffering from many heresies. Fulgentius changed directions, and instead of going to Egypt, he traveled to Rome to be able to pray at the graves of the apostles.

After a respite at Rome, Fulgentius returned in the year 500 to Byzacena, where he opened a monastery. Eight years later, the Church appointed him bishop of Ruspe. There he established another monastery, but before he could complete its construction, he and sixty other Catholic bishops were exiled by the Vandal king Thrasimund (r. 496-523) to the island of Sardinia. Thrasimund held the same heretical Arian beliefs as his Vandal predecessors Genseric (r. 428-477) and Huneric (r. 477-484). What could Fulgentius do at Sardinia? He founded a monastery. He was soon named bishop and, although he was the youngest of the island's bishops, he became their spokesman. He authored four books and several treatises on the theological errors of Arianism. In 515, Thrasimund, impressed by the persuasive arguments and humble style in which Fulgentius wrote, recalled the exile back to the mainland. Two years later, however, at the instigation of another Arian priest, the king again exiled Fulgentius to Sardinia. From 517 to 523, Fulgentius lived at the monastery that he had founded at Cagliari, in Sardinia.

When Thrasimund died in 523, Fulgentius returned to his see at Ruspe. He gently encouraged and successfully persuaded the people to eliminate the moral misconduct that had crept into their lives. At sixty-five, he retired to the island of Circinia, where he lived for a few months before returning home to Ruspe, where he died. This monk and bishop was loved and respected by all the faithful and even by many of his adversaries.

2 ✢ St. Macarius the Younger

Place: Alexandria, Egypt
Fame: Exemplary monk

Macarius the Younger (d.c. 394), also known as Macarius of Alexandria, is to be distinguished from St. Macarius the Elder, also known as Macarius of Thebes. The Younger was born and raised at Alexandria, and in young adulthood, about 335, traveled to Upper Egypt, where he remained until 373 or thereabouts, when he returned to Lower Egypt.

This monk became famous for his prayerfulness, practice of austerities, and performance of miracles. For seven years, he ate only raw vegetables and beans. Desiring to improve on this extraordinary fasting, for the next three years he consumed daily only four to five ounces of bread that he moistened with a few drops of olive oil. In order to learn from the experience of others, one Lent he traveled to the monastery headed by St. Pachomius. The visitor observed the practices of the other monks, even though his degree of austerity far surpassed theirs. Each day, he prayed while he worked, weaving palm leaves into baskets and mats. The other monks became annoyed at his singular way of working and praying. On Easter Sunday morning, they begged the abbot to send away the visitor lest he disturb further the existing standards of prayer and labor. Pachomius, too, having noticed the visitor's extraordinary behavior, discerned that the anonymous guest might be the famous Macarius. Pachomius and Macarius sat down together, whereupon Macarius revealed his identity. The pair discussed the morale of the monastery, and expressed gratitude for the time they had shared together. Then Pachomius "embraced him (Macarius), thanked him for the edification he had given, and desired him, when he returned to his desert, to offer up his prayers for them."[3]

9 ✛ St. Adrian of Canterbury

Place: North Africa
Fame: Missionary monk of England

Feeling called to the monastic life, Adrian (d. 710) left his native Africa and sailed to Naples to enter the nearby Benedictine monastery at Nerida. Renowned for his scholarship and sanctity, he was elected abbot by the monks of his monastery and was nominated to be archbishop of Canterbury by Pope Vitalian (r. 657–672). Declining the archbishopric out of humility, Adrian suggested that another monk, St. Theodore of Tarsus, be given the position and that Adrian would accompany and assist Theodore in the missionary project. The pair left Rome in 668.

En route, Adrian was detained in Gaul (now France) because the local leader suspected that the monk was carrying out a secret mission against the French on behalf of the Byzantine emperor. Released after approximately two years, Adrian continued on his way and upon his arrival Theodore appointed him abbot of the monastery of Sts. Peter and Paul, which name was changed later to the monastery of St. Augustine. There Adrian's abbacy lasted thirty-nine years.

In England, Adrian established numerous schools to educate and catechize the local population, including the School of Canterbury, which became the center of English culture.

12 ✢ St. Arcadius

Place: *Caesarea, Mauretania (now in Algeria)*
Fame: *Martyr*

In a gruesome persecution ordered by Diocletian (r. 284–305), Arcadius (d.c. 304) fled from the city to the countryside.

> The fury of the persecutors was at its height. Upon the least suspicion they broke into houses, and if they found a Christian they treated him upon the spot with the greatest cruelty, their impatience not suffering them to wait for his formal indictment. Every day new sacrileges were committed; the faithful were compelled to assist at superstitious sacrifices, to lead victims crowned with flowers through the streets, to burn incense before idols.[4]

Anticipating that he, too, would fall victim to the government's unannounced search and seizure, Arcadius fled for his life. Unfortunately, when the authorities noticed Arcadius's absence from the usual local events, they rushed to his house.

Not finding Arcadius there, the authorities took captive a relative in lieu of their intended victim.

The news reached Arcadius in his hiding place that an innocent relative was being forced to suffer what had been planned for Arcadius. Feeling compelled to free the innocent party, Arcadius returned to the city and presented himself to authorities. The judge offered freedom not only to the relative, but also to Arcadius, if he would sacrifice to the Roman gods as required by law. Arcadius refused and willingly submitted himself to the executioners.

The remainder of the story belongs to the genre of historical romance. The story continues that the judge sentenced Arcadius with the following instructions: "Let him desire death without being able to obtain it."[5] The persecutors "bid him hold out his hand, and joint after joint, chopped off his fingers, arms and shoulders. In the same barbarous manner were cut off his toes, feet, legs and thighs. The martyr voluntarily held out his limbs one after another with invincible courage, repeating, 'Lord, teach me thy wisdom.' "[6]

15 ✣ St. Macarius the Elder

Place: City of Thebes and the desert at Skete, Egypt
Fame: Founder of monastic life in the desert at Skete

Even as a youth, Macarius the Elder (c. 300-390) demonstrated the austerity and simplicity of life that later attracted numerous disciples. Preferring the solitary life, he prayed constantly as he tended cattle and wove mats in order to earn the bare necessities of life. When a woman falsely accused him of raping her, and the townspeople dragged him through the streets and beat him, he did not try to defend himself in word or action. Later, when the woman was writhing in pain during the difficult delivery of her child, she confessed the name of the real father and exonerated Macarius of any blame. The townspeople marveled at his self-composure in having borne so peacefully the false allegations and mistreatment.

At thirty, Macarius decided to live alone in the desert. Countless persons, however, followed him there, seeking either temporary counsel or lifelong discipleship. For those desiring discipleship Macarius insisted that each candidate pass the day in silence in order to converse with God instead of passing the day in idle conversation with other people. Macarius taught his disciples: "In prayer you need not use many or lofty words. You can often repeat with a sincere heart, 'Lord, show me mercy as you know best'; or, 'O God, come to my assistance.' "[7]

Austerity, Macarius taught, created the context that facilitated one's relationship with God. Macarius's most famous disciple, Evagrius, reports that the master confided to him that "for these twenty years, I have not once eaten, drunk or slept as much as nature required."[8] Macarius ate usually only once a week, and although he drank more often, he regulated his intake of wine by abstaining from it for some days if he thought that he had drunk more than his usual minimal allotment on the previous day.

The story is told that Macarius once taught another monk the virtue of indifference. The master instructed the disciple to walk to the cemetery and shout to the dead both the gravest insults and the greatest praise. When the disciple returned, Macarius inquired how the dead had responded to the shouts. When the monk replied that the deceased had made no response, "either to reproaches or praise," then Macarius advised, "Go and learn neither to be moved by abuse or by flattery. If you die to yourself and to the world, you will begin to live to Christ."[9] Numerous other stories are related about the master's insights and instructions about human nature and the spiritual life.

Controversy did not escape this solitary saint. Lucius, a usurper to the episcopal see of Alexandria, wanted to eliminate the moral support that the monks at Skete provided to the legitimately appointed bishop. Lucius' enforcers invaded the monks' hermitages and removed them to a remote island in the marshlands of the Nile delta. The intended purpose failed, however, when the monks who included not only Macarius the Elder but also St. Macarius the Younger, St. Isidore, and St. Pambo, converted at their new surroundings the pagans who had become the monks' new neighbors. Frustrated, Lucius allowed the anchorites to return to their original cells. On the way home, Macarius visited and encouraged the monks in the Nitrian desert before continuing on the way to his desert domicile at Skete. Although Macarius was not a disciple of St. Antony (also spelled Anthony), he oftentimes visited with this patriarch of all the desert monks, who lived just a fifteen days' journey east from Skete.

15 ✢ St. Isidore of Alexandria

Place: Nitrian desert and Alexandria, Egypt
Fame: Monk and hospital administrator

As a young man, Isidore of Alexandria (319-404) dedicated his life to God. Having distributed to the poor the great wealth that he had inherited from his family, he wandered into the Nitrian desert to practice the ascetical life. There he met the great bishop St. Athanasius. The two developed a master-disciple relationship. Eventually, Athanasius ordained the hermit and took him to Rome in 341. Returning to Alexandria, Isidore labored in the city's hospital and eventually became its chief administrator, spending most of his life in that position.

At age eighty, Isidore encountered a series of "persecutions, misrepresentations and troubles of every description."[10] Both the acrimonious St. Jerome and overbearing Bishop Theophilus accused Isidore of having sided with Origen, who had gained notoriety for his self-castration, for his preaching without having been ordained, and, later, for his being ordained in another diocese without having sought or received permission from his local bishop at Alexandria. Jerome harshly criticized Isidore. Theophilus, who earlier had befriended and defended Isidore, excommunicated him.

Isidore fled, first to the Nitrian desert, where he had passed many years of his youth, and later to Constantinople, where St. John Chrysostom heartily welcomed and protected the elderly priest. Isidore died in exile at Constantinople.

15 ✢ St. Paul the Hermit

Place: *Lower Thebaid desert, Egypt*
Fame: *Reputedly one of the two holiest monks of his time*

During the anti-Christian persecution of the emperor Decius (r. 249-251), twenty-one-year old Paul (c. 229-c. 342) fled to the desert. While intending only to wait out the persecution, he discovered so much joy in solitude that he remained there for the next ninety-two years. Paul's flight had been necessitated by his brother-in-law's intention to betray Paul to the political authorities. The brother-in-law hoped to inherit the estates that Paul had inherited seven years earlier, when his parents died.

Regarding the story of the famous meeting between St. Paul the first hermit and St. Antony the prototypical hermit, scholars suggest: "It seems possible, though this has been much disputed, that St. Jerome did little more than translate a Greek text of which we have versions in Syriac, Arabic and Coptic, and which contained a good deal of fabulous matter. Jerome, however, undoubtedly regarded the life as in substance historical."[11]

17 ✢ St. Antony of the Desert

Place: Thebes, Egypt
Fame: Founder of Christian monasticism

Soon after his parents died about 269, Antony (251–356) sold the family's estate and distributed the profit to the poor in order to pursue a life of solitude. His motivation was the Gospel mandate "Go, sell what you have, give it to the poor, and you shall have your treasure in heaven."[12] Taking shelter in a tomb in a local cemetery, Antony passed his days praying, performing penance, pondering the Scriptures, and reading the sacred writings of Christian authors. He writes in great detail about his battle with temptations. He earned his living by weaving and selling mats of palm fronds. His diet consisted of bread and water, three or four days a week, and never before sunset. In midlife, he added dates to his diet. In old age, he allowed himself small amounts of oil as well.

Because townsfolk kept seeking his counsel even though he kept seeking solitude, Antony moved in about 285 to Mount Pispir, atop which he isolated himself inside the walls of an abandoned fort. For twenty years, he encountered almost no one except a friend who every six months tossed bread over the walls of the fort to Antony inside. About 305, so many townsfolk and aspiring ascetics had gathered outside the fortress that, in their overwhelming desire to see him, they rushed and broke down the door of the fort. Antony exited the fort and walked among his devotees. He spoke to them in his and their native Egyptian language.

According to St. Athanasius, who was Antony's definitive biographer, the holy man exhorted the crowd to renew daily their dedication to discipleship in Jesus.

For the entire life span of men is very brief when measured against the ages to come, so that all our time is nothing in comparison with eternal life. Everything in the world is sold for what it is worth, and someone trades an item for its equivalent. But the promise of eternal life is purchased for very little. For it is written: The days of our lives have seventy years in them, but if men should be in strength, eighty years, and what is more than these would be labor and trouble. When, therefore, we live the whole eighty years, or even a hundred in the discipline, these hundred are not equal to the years we shall reign, for instead of a hundred we shall reign forever and ever. And even though we have been contestants on earth, we do not receive our inheritance on earth, but we possess the promises in heaven. Putting off the body, then, which is corruptible, we receive it back incorruptible.[13]

Antony organized these fledgling ascetics into Christianity's first monastic community. Although he did not remain permanently with the community, he occasionally visited with and instructed its members. At times, he became annoyed with himself in these journeys because he became distracted in prayer and preoccupied with his safety when crossing the crocodile-infested Arsinoitic canal. While he spoke to all sincere inquirers, he reserved his most lengthy conversations for those who evidenced truly spiritual interest and experience. He uttered only brief spiritual exhortations to worldly persons, so focused was he on spiritual depths.

This desert monk in 311 left his retreat space and traveled to the bustling metropolis of Alexandria, the second most populated city in the Roman Empire. There the final Roman anti-Christian persecution was raging and reaching its denouement. The monk comforted his best friend, Bishop Athanasius, and the persecuted flock. When Constantine ascended the throne as emperor and ceased the persecution, Antony returned to Mount

Pispir. There he organized a second community of monastics before removing himself to Mount Kolzim, near the Red Sea.

At Mount Kolzim, Antony remained in solitude for four decades, until 355, when he traveled again to the capital city to encourage Athanasius in the bitter dispute against Arianism. In his preaching, Antony exhorted Christians to be faithful to the Church, and excoriated those who had abandoned the Church in favor of the false teachings of Arius. Daily, he received visitors. Some requested prayers, while others sought instruction; some sought wisdom, and still others hoped for miraculous cures. All visitors returned, having been inspired by the hermit's holiness. The governor implored the centenarian to stay longer in the city. Antony responded, "As fish die, if they are taken from the water, so does a monk wither away if he forsakes his solitude."[14] Antony returned to Mount Kolzim, where he breathed his last.

20 ✣ Bl. Cyprian Michael Iwene Tansi

Place: *Igboezunu, Nigeria*
Fame: *Trappist monk*

When Bishop Heerey of the diocese of Onitsha in Nigeria wished to found a Trappist monastery in his diocese, he singled out the local priest Iwene Tansi (1903–1964) as the proper candidate for this ministry. Iwene accepted the invitation to pursue the "vocation within a vocation," that is, to be not only a priest, but also a Trappist priest. He agreed to travel to England, where he would train as a Trappist monk and then return to Nigeria, where he would introduce the monastic life.

Iwene had been born of humble pagan parents, the farmer Tabansi and his wife, Ejikweve. When the child Iwene went to a nearby mission school to study, the priests there called him Michael, which name he adopted at baptism at nine. At sixteen,

Iwene Michael began teaching. Six years later, he entered the seminary. At thirty-four, he was ordained a priest at the cathedral at Onitsha. As a pastor, he dedicated himself not only to daily contemplative prayer but also to active ministry. He evangelized the youth, prepared couples for marriage, visited the sick, and provided for the needs of the poor. He traveled extensively throughout the parish environs to meet and serve his people. After thirteen years as a priest, the bishop selected him as the most appropriate candidate to receive, incorporate, and share the Trappist spirituality.

Not a young man at age forty-seven, the curate left his native land and traveled to the distant land to prepare himself professionally. En route to England, Iwene Michael made a pilgrimage to Rome. In 1950, he arrived at the abbey of Mount St. Bernard at Leicestershire. Six years later, he took the religious name Cyprian.

Unfortunately, after Cyprian had begun his formation program, the Trappists reviewed the proposed location of their foundation in Africa and changed the site from Nigeria to neighboring Cameroon. Although disappointed at this change of location, Cyprian nevertheless continued his formation and dedication to the Trappist spirituality. Early in 1964, however, Cyprian was diagnosed with an aortic aneurysm. Within a few weeks, he died. Originally buried at the monastery at Leicestershire, his remains were transferred in 1988 to Onitsha and then to Aguleri, which had been his last parochial assignment in Nigeria before moving to England.

The saintliness that Cyprian Michael Iwene Tansi manifested to others had been a part of him throughout his whole life, beginning even in his youth. Commenting on his whole life, observers said, "He proved himself endowed with virtue, devoted to responsibility, and given over to piety, prayer and studies."[15]

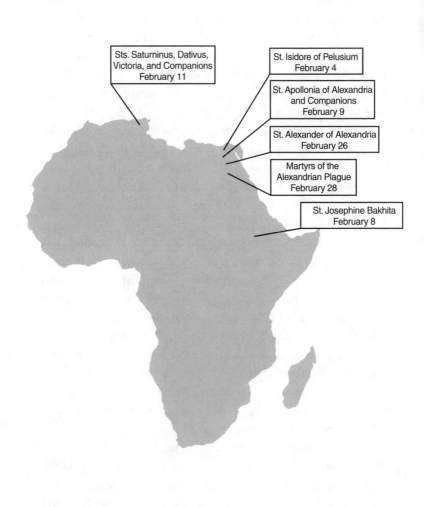

Sts. Saturninus, Dativus,
Victoria, and Companions
February 11

St. Isidore of Pelusium
February 4

St. Apollonia of Alexandria
and Companions
February 9

St. Alexander of Alexandria
February 26

Martyrs of the
Alexandrian Plague
February 28

St. Josephine Bakhita
February 8

FEBRUARY

4 ✠ St. Isidore of Pelusium

Place: Pelusium, Egypt
Fame: Abbot

Born at Alexandria, Isidore (d.c. 450) left the capital city in his youth and became a monk, priest, and abbot of the monastery of Lychnos, near Pelusium. A prolific author, Isidore wrote an estimated ten thousand letters, of which two thousand remain extant.

While entering into all the major theological and political controversies of his day, he represented the voice of moderation. He battled head-on the heresies of Nestorianism and Eutychianism, but he begged St. Cyril, the patriarch of Alexandria, in his treatment of Nestorius, not to repeat the harsh style and substance of his predecessor and uncle, Theophilus. Isidore supported St. John Chrysostom and argued against Cyril that John's name ought to be included in the Church's diptychs. Having been broadly educated in the Greek classics and in Christian theology, he appreciated the methodologies of both the Antiochene and Alexandrian schools, and opposed the use of either allegorism or historicism alone. "He refused to see a reference to Christ in every sentence of the Old Testament and maintained that while it was both historical and prophetic, it was necessary to distinguish carefully between the literal and the typical senses in interpreting that document."[1] In the spiritual life, he supported St. Paul's position that the life of virginity was to be preferred to marriage, but added that virginity lived without faithful practice of the Ten Commandments and their implied virtues benefits in no way the nonvirtuous virgin.

8 ✛ St. Josephine Bakhita

Place: Obeid, Sudan
Fame: *Emancipated slave, later a Canossian Sister of Charity*

Nine-year-old Bakhita (c. 1869-1947), playing in the fields near her home in Sudan, was captured by slave traders. She had been warned by her parents to be careful, since her older sister earlier had been captured and enslaved.

During the next ten years, the captive Bakhita passed through the hands of five different slave owners. When the first slavers captured her, she kept silent when they asked her name. In response, they named her Bakhita, which means "the lucky one." And she was lucky. She and another young girl escaped from these slavers. They ran into the woods and found freedom until a lion cornered them. The pair climbed a tree and proved more patient than the beast below. The girls' newfound freedom, however, was short-lived. Another slave trader discovered the wandering girls and took his booty to the slave market at El Obeid. The slaver decided, however, to keep Bakhita to serve as his daughter's maid.

The situation was not altogether unpleasant until one day Bakhita accidentally broke a prized vase belonging to the slaver's son. Enraged, the son demanded that the father rid the family of Bakhita. Her third owner was a Turkish military officer and his family. The women of the house mistreated Bakhita terribly, regularly beating her for no reason and tattooing her with a needle to satisfy their whim of fashion. Fortunately, this situation ended when the owner and family sold his slaves at Khartoum, from where he returned to Turkey on temporary leave. The next person to purchase the teenager was the diplomatic vice-consul for Italy at Khartoum. The man treated her kindly, and tried to relocate her with her parents. Bakhita, however, could not recall where her parents lived. When the search for her origins turned up empty, the diplomat brought Bakhita to his home at Genoa. A family friend, Signora Michieli, and her young daughter, Mimmina, grew fond of Bakhita. It was agreed that this family would become the new owner of the slave girl, who by now was fourteen.

Signora Michieli loved Bakhita and treated her well. Since the signora's wealthy family owned a hotel located near the Red Sea, it was envisioned that Bakhita eventually would travel with the family and work at the hotel as a waitress. In the meantime, the Sudanese girl was kept busy as a servant for the family's daughter.

At twenty, Bakhita prepared to leave the home at Genoa for the Red Sea hotel. Just before leaving, the family steward suggested that Bakhita ought to be instructed in the Catholic faith, and, if she wished, to be baptized. Bakhita and Mimmina took up residence at Venice in the convent of the Daughters of Charity of Canossa. From the first moment she entered the convent, Bakhita felt at home. She loved the peace and prayerfulness of the convent.

Ten months later, Signora Michieli reappeared at the door of the convent. Gently but firmly, Bakhita refused to leave. Signora insisted that Bakhita must leave, since the woman had purchased the young girl as a slave and slaves were the property of their owners. The mother superior perceived the impasse. Because Church law was involved, she called in the cardinal-patriarch, who, because civil law applied as well, called in the king's procurator. These two officials of Church and State deliberated Bakhita's future. When they asked Bakhita to state her position, she replied, "I love the Signora dearly, and to part from

Mimmina cuts me to the heart. But I shall not leave this place because I cannot risk losing God."[2] The cardinal and procurator arrived at the same decision: since slavery had been declared illegal in Italy almost a hundred years before, as soon as any foreign slave touched Italian soil, he or she immediately and automatically became freed.

Within weeks, the cardinal baptized twenty-year-old Bakhita into the Catholic Church. She rejoiced in God's love for her. Feeling loved and called by God, Bakhita expressed her desire to become a nun in the religious community of the sisters. The mother superior replied that Bakhita would be most welcomed. On December 8, 1896, she took vows of poverty, chastity, and obedience. She spent the next fifty years serving God and others in the local community houses of the Daughters of Charity of Canossa: at Venice, as portress at the Catechumenate Institute; at Schio, as cook and later as portress in the school and orphanage for girls; up and down the Italian peninsula as fund-raiser for the foreign missions. She was given the affectionate title Madre Moretta, which means "the Black Mother."

The sanctity of Bakhita was nothing extraordinary: it was not showy, but it shone through her whole life. It consisted of very down-to-earth wisdom. She had the proper word for all: for the soldiers whom she invited very clearly to go "to confess [their sins]" and for the seminarians to whom she recommended holiness. For the women who lingered around gossiping, she advised: "Go home quickly to prepare the meal, otherwise your husband will get impatient." Everyone, both great and small, was touched by her. When she went around to promote missionary vocations, she was accompanied by a Sister who did the talks. However, everyone was drawn toward Bakhita, who, going up on the platform, with few words, would manage to touch the hearts of all: "Be good, love the Lord, pray for those who do not know Him still!" Then she would make the sign of the cross and quickly go away.[3]

At the cathedral in Obeid, Sudan, a painting of Bakhita hangs next to that of the Blessed Mother, the Queen of Africa.

9 ✢ St. Apollonia of Alexandria and Companions

Place: Alexandria, Egypt
Fame: Martyred by a mob

In the last year of the reign of Roman Emperor Philip (r. 244-249), an anti-Christian mob in Alexandria unleashed its fury against innocent believers. The crazed crowd first seized the old man Metras, beat him, stuck splinters from reeds into his eyes, and then stoned him to death. Next they grabbed a woman named Quinta, whom they carried to the temple and ordered her to worship the idols there. When she refused, the blood-thirsty mob dragged her feet-first over the cobbled street to the place where they stood her upright to scourge and stone to death. When other Christians fled for their lives, the mob caught up with the elderly deaconess and virgin Apollonia (d. 249). Punching her in the face, they knocked out many of her teeth. They pulled her outside the city where a great fire was ignited. They shouted to her the options either to renounce her Christian faith or to be thrown onto the blazing pyre. The mob relented momentarily as she appeared to give consideration to their proposed alternatives. In a second, however, she threw herself onto the fire "to convince her persecutors that her sacrifice was perfectly voluntary."[4] The last victim, Serapion, was discovered in his home. The mob barged in, beat him, and took him to the rooftop, from which they hurled him headfirst to the ground, killing him.

11 ✦ Sts. Saturninus, Dativus, Victoria, and Companions

Place: *Abitina (now in Tunisia)*
Fame: *Men, women, and children martyrs*

During the reign of Diocletian (r. 284–305), magistrates and soldiers burst one Sunday morning into the church-house at Abitina, where the local Catholic community was worshiping. The government officials arrested forty-nine persons, including two senators, namely Dativus and Felix, the priest Saturninus (d. 304) and his four children, and five others identified as Ampelius, Emeritus, Rogatian, Thelica, and Victoria. The entire group of worshipers was chained and then marched to Carthage to the proconsul's residence. As the Christians marched, they sang hymns and prayed aloud to God.

At his home, the proconsul questioned the prisoners. He asked Dativus to identify himself. The senator replied that he was a Christian who had been worshiping with other Christians. The proconsul inquired perfunctorily in whose home the group gathered and who led these assemblies. Before giving Dativus a chance to answer, the proconsul ordered that the senator be placed on the rack and tortured. When questioned as to who led the group of believers, Thelica boldly replied, "The holy priest Saturninus and all of us with him."[5]

26 ✦ St. Alexander of Alexandria

Place: *Alexandria, Egypt*
Fame: *Patriarch*

Having served under the bishop St. Achillas as priest and rector of the catechetical school at Alexandria, Alexander (c. 250–328) was well prepared to succeed his mentor. As bishop himself, Alexander encountered serious challenges from three priests: Meletius of Lycopolis, who maintained an excessively strict opposition to the *lapsi* (or fallen-away Christians); Kolluthus, who usurped the bishop's power to ordain priests and deacons; and Arius, who taught that Jesus was human but not divine.

The teaching promoted by Arius created the greatest challenge to the faith and to Alexander. If Jesus were not equal to the Father, it followed that Jesus could not redeem humankind, Jesus himself was capable of sinning, and Jesus was not co-eternal. Alexander preferred gentle persuasion to authoritative pronouncement, and so the bishop took gradual steps. Because of this gentle approach Alexander suffered extreme criticism from fellow believers and severe deterioration of the theological dispute. In his early dealings with Arius, Alexander invited Arius to discuss one-on-one with the bishop their respective views on the nature of Christ. When that approach failed, Alexander asked Arius to meet not only with the bishop, but also all the clergy of the diocese to arrive at a common understanding of the Church's teaching. In that assembly, when Arius remained incorrigible in his position, Alexander required Arius to appear before all the bishops of Egypt joined in council. Finally, the bishops, under the leadership of Alexander, condemned and excommunicated the obstinate priest.

A propaganda battle ensued. Alexander sent letters to bishops protesting the teachings of Arius. The emperor in the East, Constantine I (r. 307-337), wishing to avoid internal ecclesiastical divisions, sent Bishop Hosius of Córdoba to Alexandria to request that Alexander and Arius sit down together and reconcile their differences. Alexander quickly won Hosius to his point of view. The patriarch convened another synod of all Egyptian bishops, who again failed to win over the recalcitrant Arius. Both Hosius and Alexander agreed to seek a general council to which all the bishops of the Church would be invited. This council, held at Nicaea in 325, declared that Jesus was true God and true man, one person with two natures. The council affirmed the Egyptian bishops' prior excommunication of Arius and banished him.

Although Alexander had won the day, the Church at Alexandria had little peace. Arianism continued its rapid rise throughout the Church, especially in Egypt. Alexander's successor, St. Athanasius, continued the theological battle that Alexander had waged so courageously and convincingly in local, regional, and ecumenical councils.

28 ✢ Martyrs of the Alexandrian Plague

Place: Alexandria, Egypt
Fame: Humble servants of the sick and dying

Pestilence raged throughout the greater part of the Roman Empire during the years 249 to 263. In Rome, five thousand persons are said to have died in one day and Alexandria in particular suffered severely: St. Dionysius of Alexandria tells us that his city had already been afflicted with famine, and this was followed by tumults and violence so uncontrolled that it was safer to travel from one extremity of the known world to the other than to go from one street of Alexandria to the next. To these scourges succeeded the plague, which raged until there was not one house in that great city that escaped or which had not some death to mourn. Corpses lay unburied, and the air was laden with infection, mingled with pestilential vapours from the Nile. The living appeared wild with terror, and the fear of death rendered the pagan citizens cruel to their nearest relations; as soon as anyone was known to have caught the infection, his friends fled from him: the bodies of those not yet dead were thrown into the streets and abandoned.[6]

In this situation, Christians responded with the greatest charity. Despite the fact that previously their members had been tortured, exiled, and slain, the community responded in caring physically and spiritually for those for whom no one else cared.

Most of the brethren were prodigal in their love and brotherly kindness. They supported one another, visited the sick fearlessly, and looked after them without stint, serving them in Christ. They were happy to die with them, bearing their neighbours' burdens and taking their disease and pain on themselves, even to the death which they caught from them. They put reality into what we look on as a courteous formula, accepting death as "humble servants" of one another.

The best among our brethren died in this way, including several priests and deacons and those men and women who were most looked up to. Thus to bring oneself to the grave evinced such religious dutifulness and strength of faith that it seemed, indeed, not to fall short of martyrdom itself.

With their own bare hands, they closed the eyes and mouths of the saints; they carried their bodies away and laid them out; they embraced and kissed them, washed them and put on their grave-clothes. And it was not very long before they were tended in the same way themselves, for the survivors were continually following those who had already been taken. But the heathen behaved very differently.[7]

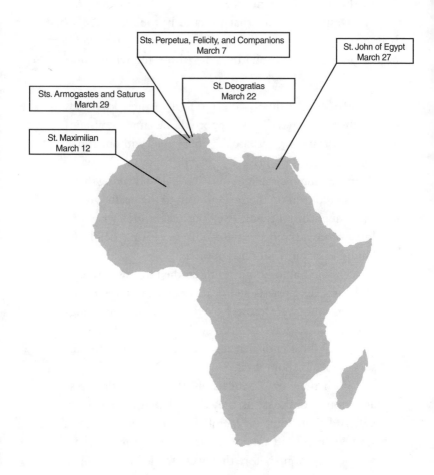

Sts. Perpetua, Felicity, and Companions
March 7

St. John of Egypt
March 27

Sts. Armogastes and Saturus
March 29

St. Deogratias
March 22

St. Maximilian
March 12

MARCH

7 ✛ Sts. Perpetua, Felicity, and Companions

Place: Carthage (now in Tunisia)
Fame: Young mothers martyred in the early Church

Five catechumens — the nursing mothers Perpetua (d. 203) and Felicity (d. 203), the slave Revocatus, and Saturninus and Secundulus — died for the Christian faith at the amphitheater at Carthage. Their instructor in the faith, Saturus, voluntarily joined them in prison, baptized them there, and suffered martyrdom with them.

The Roman emperor and African native Septimus Severus (r. 193-211) had decreed that whoever would refuse to offer sacrifice in his honor would be thrown to the wild animals. After the five catechumens were arrested, they were placed, according to custom, under house arrest, whereby they were allowed to receive visitors. Perpetua's father brought her infant son to her and begged her by his outpouring of emotions and arguments to reconsider her decision. Perpetua's autobiographical account follows.

"When we were still with our guards (at Thurburbo)," she says, "my father in his affection for me was trying to upset me by arguments and to overthrow my resolution." "Father," I said, "Do you see this vessel lying here, a waterpot or whatever it may be?" "I see it," he said. "Can it be called by any other name than what it is?" "No," he answered. "So also I cannot call myself anything else than what I am, a Christian." Then my father, furious at the word Christian, threw himself upon me as though to pluck out my eyes; but he was satisfied with annoying me; he was in fact vanquished, he and his devil's arguments. . . . A few days later we were transferred to the prison (in Carthage). I was terrified, because I have never known such darkness. What a day of horror! Suffocating heat from the crowds, rough handling by the soldiers. To crown all I was tormented there by anxiety for my baby. Then Tertius and Pomponius, those devoted deacons who were ministering to us, paid for us to be removed for a few hours to a better part of the prison and refresh ourselves. At that point all the detainees left the cell and did as they pleased. I suckled my baby, who was dying of hunger.[1]

Nothing was ever reported about the infant boy's father; we do not know his name, his whereabouts, or whether he was dead or alive. And Secundulus died in prison prior to the examination before Hilarion.

After some days under house arrest, without warning, the two women and three surviving men were brought to trial. The local procurator, Hilarion, interrogated them. Encouraging Perpetua to deny her faith, he said, "Spare your father's gray hairs; spare your boy's tender years. Offer sacrifice for the emperor's welfare."[2] She, however, refused to renege on her faith.

In prison, while the noblewoman Perpetua had been nursing her son, the slave woman Felicity gave birth to a daughter. Soon the two women had to hand the two infants to family members. The five captives were transferred to a public prison, where passersby gawked at and ridiculed the incarcerated Christians. Perpetua continues her account:

Because I was anxious about him [her son], I spoke to my mother. Then I comforted my brother, commending my son to their charge. I was suffering a great deal because I saw them suffer on my account. These anxieties tormented me for many days. Eventually I obtained permission for my baby to remain in the prison with me; and at once he regained his health and I was relieved of my trouble and the anxiety he had caused me. My prison suddenly became a palace to me, and I would rather have been there than anywhere else.[3]

After some days of imprisonment, the five were brought roughly to the amphitheater. There a leopard, a bear, and a wild boar mauled to death the three men. A wild cow attacked and trampled the two women. An eyewitness reports:

For the women the keepers had a savage cow ready, an unusual animal, chosen in mockery of their sex. They were stripped and wrapped in nets, and when they were thus brought out the people were shocked at the sight, the one a graceful girl, the other fresh from childbirth with milk dripping from her breasts. So they were brought back and clothed in loose gowns. First Perpetua was tossed. She sat up and drew her torn tunic about her, being more mindful of shame than of pain; and then she tidied her tumbled hair, for it was not seemly that a martyr should suffer with hair disheveled, lest she should appear to mourn in her glory. Then she got up and went to help Felicity, who had been knocked down, and they were both called back to the Sanavivaria gate. Perpetua, "so lost was she in the Spirit and ecstasy," looked around and to everyone's astonishment asked when they were to be thrown to the cow. Only her bruises and torn dress persuaded her that it had already happened. Then she turned to her brother and another catechumen and said to them, "Stand fast in the faith and love one another. And do not let what we suffer be a stumbling-block to you."[4]

Having witnessed the women's sufferings, the crowd at first chanted for the release of the injured women, but the fickle mob soon changed its chant and clamored for the women's deaths. Whereas the men had died outright, the two wounded women willingly walked to the center of the amphitheater, where the gladiators waited to kill off their victims. Perpetua's killer, however, missed her heart with his first thrust, so shrieking with pain, she guided "to her own throat the sword of her nervous executioner, who had failed to kill her at the first stroke."[5]

The written account of these martyrs was composed by three eyewitnesses, namely Perpetua herself, Saturus himself, and a third person who many scholars surmise was the renowned Christian apologist Tertullian. The record of these martyrs became so popular in the early Church that Augustine warned against their being used on a par with the Sacred Scriptures.

12 ✣ St. Maximilian

Place: Numidia (now in Algeria)
Fame: Conscientious objector

During the persecution ordered by Diocletian (r. 284–305), the Christian youth Maximilian (274–295) was conscripted to serve in the Roman army. Because he refused to be drafted into the military, he was summoned to court. Maximilian appeared with his father, Fabius Victor. Maximilian was measured for the army; he measured five feet ten inches. Then the proconsul Dion offered the young Christian the opportunity to reconsider his decision. Maximilian remained steadfast. "The *passio* of St. Maximilian is one of that small collection of precious documents that is an authentic, contemporary and practically unembroidered account of the trial and death of an early martyr."[6] The following dialogue took place.

Dion: You must serve or die.

Maximilian: I will never serve. You can cut off my head, but I will not be a soldier of this world, for I am a soldier of Christ.

Dion: What has put these ideas into your head?

Maximilian: My conscience and He who has called me.

Dion (to Fabius Victor): Put your son right.

Victor: He knows what he believes and he will not change.

Dion (to Maximilian): Be a soldier and accept the emperor's badge.

Maximilian: Not at all. I carry the mark of Christ my God already.

Dion (to the recruiting officer): Give him his badge.

Maximilian: I will not take the badge. If you insist, I will deface it. I am a Christian, and I am not allowed to wear that leaden seal round my neck. For I already carry the sacred sign of the Christ, the Son of the living God, whom you know not, the Christ who suffered for our salvation, whom God gave to die for our sins. It is He whom all we Christians serve, it is He whom we follow, for He is the Lord of life, the Author of our salvation.

Dion: Join the service and accept the seal, or else you will perish miserably.[7]

The conversation continued with neither side yielding any ground. Finally, Dion sentenced Maximilian to death by beheading on the charge of refusing to take the military oath. Immediately, a soldier reached out and decapitated the young man with his father standing right beside him. Maximilian's last words were, "The fruits of this good work will be multiplied an hundredfold. May I welcome you in Heaven and glorify God with you."[8] A Christian woman arranged to transport the body of Maximilian to Carthage, where Maximilian was laid to rest near the grave site of Bishop Cyprian, who had been martyred thirty-seven years previously.

22 ✠ St. Deogratias

Place: Carthage (now in Tunisia)
Fame: Pastoral bishop

For fourteen years, ever since the Vandal king Genseric (r. 428-477) had conquered Carthage in 439, the proconsular province's capital city suffered without a bishop. Finally, the emperor Valentinian III (r. 424-455) urged the king to promote someone to that see. Genseric chose the priest Deogratias (d. 457), who by his charity and preaching already enjoyed the support of local Catholic congregations. Two years after Deogratias' episcopal ordination, Genseric invaded Rome and brought back as booty to the northern African coastal city thousands of captives. For three years, Deogratias dedicated his life to responding to the practical and spiritual needs of these victims.

> When the throng of captives reached the shore of Africa, the Vandals and Moors divided the huge mass of people into groups. Husbands were separated from wives and children from their parents, in accordance with the custom of the barbarians. That beloved man [Deogratias] who was filled with God busied himself immediately. He sold all the gold and silver vessels used in worship and freed the freeborn people from being slaves of the barbarians, so that spouses would remain together and

children be returned to the parents. And because there were no places large enough to hold such a throng, he set aside the two sizeable basilicas we have named, that of Faustus and that of the Novae, with beds and straw, deciding each day how much it was proper for each person to receive.

Because most of them had been weakened by sailing, an experience with which they were unfamiliar, and by the harshness of their captivity, there was no small number of sick people among them. That blessed bishop acted like a good nurse. He continually went on rounds with the doctors, and food was brought behind him, so that when each person's pulse had been taken, that person might be given what was needed, in his presence. He did not even rest from this merciful work in the hours of night, but he went on, hurrying from bed to bed, enquiring as to how each was doing. So it was that he took on himself every burden, sparing neither his weary limbs nor his decayed old age.[9]

The Vandals grew angry at Deogratias' assistance to the captives and his ever-increasing popularity among both Arians and Catholics. Some Vandals attempted to kill him, but the bishop's own exhaustion from service ended Deogratias' life.

27 ✢ St. John of Egypt

Place: Lycopolis in Lower Thebaid, Egypt
Fame: Monk and miracle worker

Between the ages of twenty-five and thirty, John (304-394) forsook his occupation as a carpenter in order to become a monk. He placed himself under the tutelage of an elderly local hermit, who imposed strict and sometimes strange acts of obedience. "John obeyed unquestioningly, however unreasonable the task imposed: for a whole year, at the command of his spiritual father, he daily watered a dry stick as though it had been a live plant and carried out other equally ridiculous orders."[10] After about ten years of this discipleship, the old anchorite died, and John spent approximately five years visiting other monasteries in Egypt.

At about age forty, John moved to a remote cave on Mount Lycos, near his native Lycopolis. There he established in the rock three adjoining chambers: a prayer room, a bedroom, and a combination workroom and living room. He isolated himself from the outside world. He created only a small opening through which he received offerings of fruits and vegetables, and the prayer requests of visitors. He prayed privately all week long, except on Saturday and Sunday, when he received male, but never female, visitors. He never ate until sunset, and his diet consisted of only dried fruits and vegetables. John kept this pattern of living for about the next fifty years.

John's visitors attested to his ability to heal the sick, read people's hearts, and predict the outcome of future events. "Of his many prophecies the most celebrated were those made to the Emperor Theodosius I."[11] In 388 and 392, the emperor sent his legates from Constantinople deep into the desert of Egypt to locate John and seek his foretelling regarding the emperor's proposed battles. In the first case, John said the emperor would defeat his enemies. The emperor marched and won the war. In the second case, John warned that the emperor would win his war, but that he would not long survive the contest. The emperor won the war, but died six months later.

St. Jerome, St. Augustine, St. Palladius, and St. John Cassian all praised John in their writings of the Desert Fathers.

29 ✠ Sts. Armogastes and Saturus

Place: Carthage (now in Tunisia)
Fame: Martyrs at the hands of the Vandals

These two martyrs died during one of the many periods of the Vandals' anti-Catholic persecutions. Genseric (r. 428–477) had decreed that only Arians and no Catholics were permitted to hold positions of employment in the king's and his families' courts and households. Armogastes and Saturus (who both died around 455), however, already had been working in the households, respectively of Genseric's son Theodoric and Genseric's father, Huneric. Due to Genseric's decree both men were relieved of their employment and were punished for practicing the Catholic faith.

Armogastes's initial punishment consisted of having his shins and forehead tied tightly with strings of hemp. When this torture failed, the Vandals devised other ways to punish Armogastes.

> As the holy man looked toward heaven the strings were broken as if they were the threads of spiders' webs. When the torturers saw that the strings that had bound him were broken, they kept on bringing stronger strings and pieces of hemp, but he simply invoked the name of Christ and they were all as nothing. Moreover, while he was made to hang with head downwards, supported by one foot, everyone saw him sleeping as if her were on a feather bed.[12]

So frustrated was the king's son Theodoric that he wanted to behead Armogastes there and then. The Arian priest-advisers dissuaded the prince because "the Romans will begin to preach that he is a martyr."[13] Instead, Armogastes was exiled to the province of Byzacena, where he was ordered to dig ditches for new vines. As if to increase the martyr's shame, he was brought back to the outskirts of Carthage, where everybody would see him reduced to a cowherd. Armogastes accepted his physical sufferings and intended humiliations in a way that endeared him to the hearts of the Catholics and inspired them to keep the faith.

Saturus had served as superintendent of Huneric's household. After the promulgation of the decree restricting employment in the king's households to Arians, the Catholic Saturus was offered a choice.

> Honours and wealth in abundance were promised if he did this (convert to Arianism); dire punishments were to be prepared if he refused. This was the choice placed before him: if he did not obey the king's commands, an examination was to be conducted. First of all he would lose his house and wealth, and all his slaves and children would be sold; then, while he was present, his wife would be given in marriage to a camel driver.[14]

The old man could not be swayed by bribery or threats. He reaffirmed his faith and rejected the offer of conversion. His wife, however, grew desperate. She came to him where he was praying in the middle of the night. "She had rent her garments and let down her hair; their children were with her and she carried in her hands a little girl who was still at the breast. She placed her at the feet of her unknowing husband, while she herself embraced his knees with her arms." [15] She begged her husband to reconsider his decision. He replied with the words of the Gospel, "If anyone does not give up his wife, children, fields or house, he cannot be my disciple."[16]

At the planned investigation, Saturus was found guilty of being Catholic. He was forbidden ever to appear again in public and was banished to the wilderness.

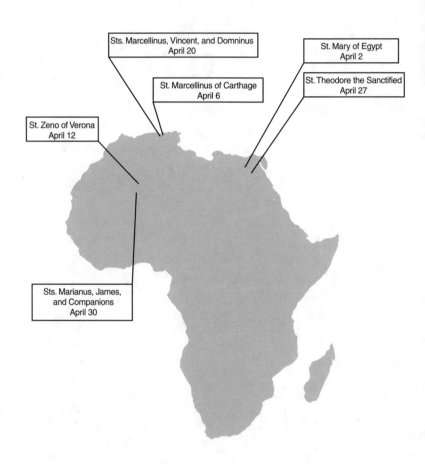

St. Benedict the Moor
April 4
SICILY

Sts. Marcellinus, Vincent, and Domninus
April 20

St. Mary of Egypt
April 2

St. Marcellinus of Carthage
April 6

St. Theodore the Sanctified
April 27

St. Zeno of Verona
April 12

Sts. Marianus, James,
and Companions
April 30

APRIL

2 ✢ St. Mary of Egypt

Place: *Alexandria, Egypt*
Fame: *Pagan courtesan who became a Christian hermit*

A credible story grew into an incredible legend in the case of
Mary of Egypt (d. fifth century). The kernel of truth is that two
disciples of St. Cyriacus discovered a woman hiding in the otherwise uninhabited desert beyond the Jordan River. As she ran
away into the bushes, the two men followed her and successfully traced her steps until they discovered her hiding in a cave.
When they spoke with her, the woman explained that at twelve
years of age, she had left home and traveled to Alexandria, where
she found employment as a singer and dancer. After many years
in her profession, she fled from the city to the desert to make
amends for the sins of her former way of life. Cyriacus's two
disciples returned to him and reported what they had seen and
heard. Eventually all three men went out into the desert in
search of Mary. When they came upon her, they discovered that
she had died, and buried her. Cyril of Scythopolis reports this
credible story in his early fifth-century biography of the life of
St. Cyriacus.

The basic outline of this story was expanded two centuries
later by St. Sophronius, the patriarch of Jerusalem. A hundred
years later, St. John Damascene apparently accepted the story as
true and quoted at great length from Sophronius's story of Mary
of Egypt.

Sophronius reports that Mary's story occurred in 430, in
the reign of Theodosius the Younger (r. 408–450) at Palestine.

He writes that a priest named St. Zosimus, after fifty-three years as a monk, decided to develop further his life with God by living for one year away from the comfort of his house in the wilds of the Jordanian desert. In the wilderness, he found shelter with a community of monks. Their custom was to leave their cells and wander in the desert for five weeks between the first Sunday of Lent and Passion (or Palm) Sunday. While Zosimus was in the desert, a twenty-day journey from his monastery, he sat down at noon to pray the psalms and in the distance he saw what appeared to be a human figure. As he approached, the person ran away. Zosimus pursued the fellow hermit.

On the verge of being overtaken, the fleeing figure stopped, turned to Zosimus, and begged him to come no nearer. The figure identified herself as a woman, who begged for his cloak, since she was poorly clad. She explained that she was an Egyptian, who had run away from home without her parents' consent when she was twelve. Full of words of shame, she admitted that she had fallen into prostitution, and regretted the first steps that had taken her down that path. At twenty-eight, she joined a band of pilgrims journeying to Jerusalem. Along the way, she continued her habitual behavior, seducing some of the pilgrims. At Jerusalem, she attempted to enter the church of the Holy Sepulchre, but some invisible power held her back. Three times she tried to enter, but three times she was thrown back. At last, looking up, she spotted an icon of the Blessed Virgin Mary. Breaking into tears, Mary of Egypt wept and confessed her sins. Freed from shame and guilt, she was freed to enter the church. Upon leaving the church, she stopped before the icon, where she received the revelation to go to the Jordanian desert to do penance. There she passed the next forty-seven years, living on edible plants and dates. Zosimus promised not to tell anyone about her story as long as she was alive.

The following year, on Holy Thursday, the two met as

planned, whereupon Zosimus gave Mary Holy Communion. The second year, Zosimus went as planned, but Mary was lying dead at the meeting spot. A note beside her explained that she had died on the past Good Friday, and asked if he would bury her. Zosimus prayed over her, then buried her. Taking back the cloak that he had given her two years previously, he regarded the garment as a relic. Returning to the monastery, he told his fellow monks this story, which is left up to contemporary readers to determine whether it is completely factual or whether some parts are fictitious.

4 ✠ St. Benedict the Moor

Place: *Palermo, Sicily*
Fame: *Patron of African-Americans in North America*

The parents of Benedict (1526-1589) were brought as slaves from Africa to Sicily. They converted to Christianity and took the Christian names Christopher and Diana and the family name Manasseri, which was the surname of the landowner for whom they worked at Messina.

Benedict grew up on the farm, a slave like his parents. When he celebrated his eighteenth birthday, Benedict was freed from slavery. This manumission fulfilled a promise the slave owner had made to Benedict's father that his oldest son would be released from slavery as compensation for the father's having served as foreman of all the field hands.

Finding work as a day laborer, Benedict earned a meager wage that he shared with people of lesser means. He also volunteered to care for the sick. During his youth, he had earned the reputation and the nickname *"il moro santo,"* that is, "the black saint," which has been mistranslated as "the Moor," incorrectly identifying Benedict's ethnic and religious roots.

Feeling called to dedicate his life to God, Benedict joined a band of hermits in 1547. Their leader was Jerome Lanza, a former local nobleman, who had sold all he had and distributed his wealth to the poor to lead a life of poverty and prayer. Benedict followed suit and joined the hermits in the hillsides surrounding San Fratello. The hermits, seeking ever greater solitude, moved their quarters many times and eventually settled at Montepellegrino, near Palermo. When Lanza died, the group elected Benedict their leader. In 1562, however, Pope Pius IV ordered all bands of loosely organized hermits either to disband or to join established religious orders. Benedict joined the Order of Friars Minor of the Observance at the Friary of St. Mary of Jesus at Palermo. He remained there for the next twenty-four years.

As a friar, Benedict's first assignment was to serve as cook at the friary at Palermo. While serving others, he won a reputation for reading people's hearts, giving wise advice, responding compassionately to the needs of the poor, and working miracles. In 1578, although he was a lay brother and not ordained, he was named the guardian of the friary and shortly thereafter the novice master for the young candidates. After some few years in these positions, he asked to be removed so that he could return to his original responsibility as cook.

> He was glad when he was released and allowed to return to the kitchen, although his position was scarcely that of the obscure cook of earlier years. Now, all day long, he was beset by visitors of all conditions — the poor demanding alms, the sick seeking to be healed, and distinguished persons requesting his advice or his prayers. Though he never refused to see those who asked for him, he shrank from marks of respect, and when traveling would cover his face with his hood and if possible

chose the night that he might not be recognized. Throughout his life he continued the austerities of his hermit days.[1]

After suffering a brief illness, he died. He was buried where he had spent the last thirty-six years of his life. His incorrupt body still remains there.

6 ✢ St. Marcellinus of Carthage

Place: Carthage (now in Tunisia)
Fame: Papal legate and martyr

As secretary of state to Emperor Honorius (r. 395–423), Marcellinus (d. 413) was sent to Carthage to resolve a dispute between the Catholics and Donatists. Marcellinus decided in favor of the Catholics. He brutally enforced the decision. The Donatists alleged that Marcellinus was a protagonist in the Heraclian rebellion. The general Marinus proceeded to capture Marcellinus, imprison him, and execute him. The emperor severely criticized Marinus. Augustine dedicated his *City of God* to his dear friend Marcellinus. A question remains whether he was a native African.

12 ✢ St. Zeno of Verona

Place: Iol Caesarea, Mauretania (now Cherchell, Algeria)
Fame: Innovative and effective bishop of Verona, Italy

"From a panegyric he delivered on St. Arcadius, a Mauretanian martyr, it has been conjectured that St. Zeno (d.c. 371) was born in Africa."[2] In approximately 362, Zeno was named bishop of Verona. "We gather a number of interesting particulars about him and his people from a collection of his *tractati*, which are short discourses delivered to his flock."[3]

The bishop congratulated his people on their great generosity in caring for the practical needs of their neighbors and the Church. When neighbors experienced needs of food and shelter, Church members responded swiftly. When the growing congregation needed more space in which to worship, the members gave generously to support the construction of a basilica. Zeno's writings reveal a number of the bishop's practices conducted during Holy Week. At that time, he normally ordained priests, reconciled penitents, and baptized many persons. At the Easter Vigil, the bishop provided a large baptismal pool into which the candidates entered and were completely immersed. Long before a contemporary, St. Ambrose, formed convents of women at Milan, this bishop formed a society of veiled women who dedicated themselves to God and to a life of virginity. Some of these women remained at home, while others gathered together in a convent.

Zeno zealously preached and wrote against both paganism and Arianism, and won numerous persons to the Catholic religion. In his own church, he confronted the scandalous abuses of the agape (or love feast) and the practice of excessive shrieking and crying out during funeral services.

20 ✛ Sts. Marcellinus, Vincent, and Domninus

Place: *Proconsular Africa (now in Algeria, Tunisia, and Libya)*
Fame: *Missionary bishop to Dauphine region in Gaul (now France)*

Marcellinus (d.c. 374) with two fellow missionaries, St. Vincent and St. Domninus, left their native Africa to evangelize in Gaul in the area that later became known as the Dauphine region of France. The small edifice that had begun as the missionaries' chapel was expanded later by Marcellinus to make room for the many local converts from paganism to Christianity. The Gallic metropolitan archbishop, St. Eusebius of Vercelli, appointed Marcellinus the first bishop of Embrun because of the missionary's zeal for souls and reputation for holiness. In the later years of life, Marcellinus suffered verbal and physical persecution from the Arians. These attacks eventually forced the aged bishop to flee for his life. He hid in the Auvergne Mountains and occasionally dared, under the cover of night, to return to Embrun to assist members of his congregation.

27 ✤ St. Theodore the Sanctified

Place: Egypt
Fame: Monk, disciple of Pachomius

Around his twelfth birthday, Theodore (c. 314–368) committed his life to God. Later on, he left home to make himself a disciple to the famous St. Pachomius at Tabennisi. This Father among the monks recognized the extraordinary gifts of Theodore, promoted him to priesthood, and made him his protégé on visitations to surrounding monasteries.

Succession to Pachomius presented a problem. The great abbot had designated Petronius to succeed him. Unfortunately, Petronius died thirteen days after his predecessor. The monks then chose St. Orsiesius, but many members of the group soon became disgruntled with his leadership. Not wishing to remain a cause of division and object of complaint, Orsiesius stepped down after having appointed Theodore as the new abbot.

Theodore restored peace to the monasteries. "He assembled the monks, exhorted them to unanimity, inquired into the cause of the divisions and applied effectual remedies. By his prayers and endeavours union and charity were restored. St. Theodore visited the monasteries one after another, and instructed, comforted, and encouraged every monk in particular, correcting faults with a sweetness which gained the heart."[4]

Numerous predictions were attributed to him. One time, while riding on the Nile River with the five-times exiled archbishop St. Athanasius, Theodore assured the Church leader that his nemesis, Emperor Julian the Apostate (r. 361–363), had died that very day and that the new emperor would end the persecution against the Church. Both foretellings soon were confirmed.

It is claimed that Theodore possessed the power to perform miracles.

> One of St. Theodore's miracles provides an early example of the use of blessed water as a sacramental for the healing of body and soul. The story is told by a contemporary — St. Ammon. A man came to the monastery at Tabennisi, asking St. Theodore to come and pray over his daughter, who was sick. Theodore was not able to go, but reminded the man that God could hear his prayers wherever they were offered. To which the man replied that he had not a great faith, and brought a silver vessel of water, asking the monk that he would at least invoke the name of God upon that so it might be as a medicine for her. Then Theodore prayed and made the sign of the cross over the water, and the man took it home. He found his daughter unconscious, so he forced open her mouth and poured some of it down her throat. And by virtue of the prayer of St. Theodore the girl was saved and recovered her health.[5]

Theodore's special powers to foretell the future and to heal the sick confirmed for his contemporaries that he was especially blessed by God. Theodore the Sanctified is also called Theodore of Tabennisi.

30 ✢ Sts. Marianus, James, and Companions

Place: Cirta, Numidia (now in Algeria)
Fame: Lector and deacon martyrs

The lector Marianus and deacon James (d. 259) were very cruelly mistreated. This pair — along with two bishops (Agapius and Secundinus), two women (Tertulla and Antonia), a nobleman (Aemilian), and countless other Christians — were arrested and tortured in the province of Numidia in or near the city of Cirta, which is now Constantine. Marianus's penalty consisted of his being hanged by his thumbs with weights attached to his feet before being beheaded during the persecution of Emperor Valerian (r. 253-260).

After the governor interrogated them, the group was force-marched eighty miles south to the city of Lambesa. Marianus reported a vision of the martyred Bishop Cyprian welcoming him into heaven, and James shared a dream of an angelic figure calling him to "follow me quickly."[6] "An account of their passion was written, at their own request, for the information and encouragement of their brethren in faith by an anonymous writer who knew them extremely well and for a time shared their imprisonment."[7] An excerpt follows.

> They were led to a hollow in a river valley, where the high ground on either side served for seats, as in a theatre. The river running through the midst received the blood of the blessed: two kinds of baptism were seen there, by blood and by water. So many were the holy victims that they were drawn up in rows, and the executioner passed with swift fury from one to the next, striking off their heads; thus he lightened his burdensome task and carried it out tidily and with dispatch.[8]

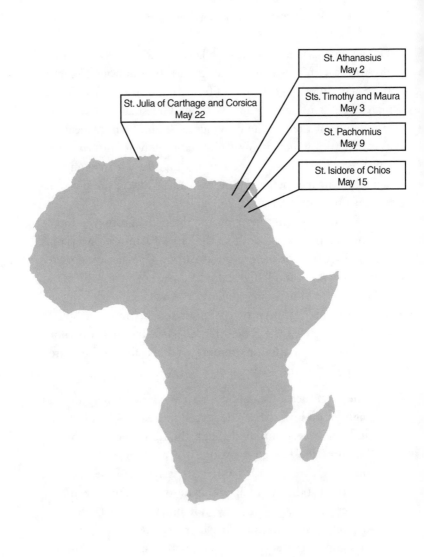

St. Athanasius
May 2

Sts. Timothy and Maura
May 3

St. Pachomius
May 9

St. Isidore of Chios
May 15

St. Julia of Carthage and Corsica
May 22

MAY

2 ✞ St. Athanasius

Place: *Alexandria, Egypt*
Fame: *Doctor and Father of the Church, prolific author*

Few churchmen have manifested the constant courage and have endured the lifelong attacks that Athanasius (c. 297–373) suffered. Over a period of seventeen years, he was exiled five times by four different emperors and was condemned by three Church councils dominated by his enemies. Despite the constant controversy in his life, or perhaps because of his positive responses to these challenges, he has been named a Father and Doctor of the Church.

Athanasius' Christian parents provided him with an excellent education in classical subjects and Christian theology. He was instructed in the faith by teachers who believed strongly enough to confess their faith during persecution. As a youth, he became a disciple of St. Antony, the famous centenarian monk of the desert. At twenty-one, Athanasius began theological studies. Seven years later, he was ordained a deacon. His first assignment was to serve as secretary to the great archbishop St. Alexander of Alexandria.

Already at Alexandria, trouble was brewing over Arianism. The priest Arius had begun teaching as early as 323 a new doctrine that Jesus was not equal with the Father, but was created by the Father; therefore, Jesus was not truly God. Arius's bishop Alexander requested and received from Arius a written statement of his novel teaching and presented this information first to the local clergy and eventually to a council of Egyptian bishops, who listened and then condemned the ideas and the man. Arius left Egypt and went north to Caesarea, where he continued to propagate his teachings, with the approval of Bishop Eusebius of Nicomedia.

This theological turmoil gave rise to the critical Council of Nicaea in 325. Athanasius attended in his role as secretary to Alexander, but the young priest did not participate as a voting member. The council defined the Church's belief in the relationship between the divine and human in Jesus, that is, that Jesus is truly God and truly man, having two natures in the one person. When Athanasius returned to the capital city in 328, he was named bishop of the see.

In 330, Eusebius, the powerful archbishop of Nicomedia, wrote to both the emperor Constantine (r. 307-337) and Athanasius urging them to reinstate Arius to the ranks of the clergy in Alexandria. Theological issues involved both the political and religious leaders. Constantine ordered the appointment, but Athanasius responded that Arius had broken his bond with the Church by spreading false teachings. Eusebius then conspired with the Meletians at Egypt to bring formal charges against Athanasius. The charges consisted of misusing Church monies, committing treason against the emperor, and destroying the chalice used by a Meletian priest. Athanasius traveled to Constantinople to defend himself in front of Emperor Constantine, who heard the case and dropped all charges.

No sooner had Athanasius arrived home at Alexandria than the Meletians charged him with having murdered a Meletian bishop, whom "everyone knew was alive and in hiding."[1] Although summoned to appear at a council in Caesarea to answer the murder charge, the bishop ignored the summons and stayed home. In 335, he was summoned again to another council, this time at Tyre, to answer a whole new series of charges. He went in good faith, but discovered there that the council was packed with his enemies. Athanasius requested and received a recess to gather evidence for his case. Instead, he fled to Constantinople, where he threw himself at the mercy of the emperor and begged for a hearing. The emperor listened and wrote a letter vindicating Athanasius of all charges. Overnight, however, and without explanation, Emperor Constantine changed his mind. He now exiled Athanasius to the western frontier city of Trier, which was located near the Rhine River in faraway Gaul. While in exile in the Western empire, Athanasius introduced there the monasticism he had learned from the desert monks in the Eastern empire.

Exile lasted two-and-a-half years until the emperor died. Constantine's empire was then divided among his three sons: Constantine II (r. 337-340), Constantius (r. 337-361), and Constans (r. 337-350); Constantine II revoked the exile of Athanasius in the West. Constantius, however, in whose territory lay Alexandria, refused to restore Athanasius. Instead, he charged Athanasius with fomenting civil unrest. A synod was convened at Rome to hear the case. Athanasius' detractors never showed up at the trial. Vindicated but not yet victorious, Athanasius could not return home. A usurper had claimed the bishop's see.

Eight years later, when the usurper died, Athanasius returned to Alexandria amid great rejoicing by members of his flock. A change in political circumstances, but not a change of heart, had effected Athanasius' return. One of the defenders of Athanasius, Constans, was needed by his brother Constantius II in a war being waged against Persia. As soon as Constans died in battle, however, Constantius II declared that he would eliminate Athanasius from the realm. The emperor convened Church councils in 353 at Arles and 355 at Milan, "where he declared himself to be the accuser of Athanasius."[2] The emperor-compliant bishops then exiled all the Catholic bishops, including Pope Libellius, who also eventually acquiesced to the emperor's vendetta against, and exile of, Athanasius.

Back in Egypt, Athanasius felt safely protected by his supporters until members of the emperor's army crashed through the church doors during Mass. While approaching Athanasius, the soldiers slashed and killed row after row of worshipers, which delay enabled Athanasius to escape. He fled to the desert and hid there, moving from place to place for six years. While in exile in the Egyptian desert, he wrote prolifically about the incarnation of Jesus, the errors of Arius, and spiritual treatises about his own flight and desert experiences.

When Constantius died in 361, the new emperor, Julian the Apostate (r. 361–363), recalled Athanasius. This respite lasted only four months because the archbishop refused to cooperate with the emperor's plan to reinstate the pagan religion in the empire. Again, Athanasius was sent packing by the emperor. The bishop fled to the desert and narrowly escaped capture by the emperor's soldiers. This fourth exile ended when Julian was killed in the war at Persia.

Julian's successor, Jovian (r. 363–364), an ardent Christian, recalled Athanasius. Unfortunately, Jovian died within a year and a half. Valens (r. 364–378) became the new emperor and immediately reverted to the policies of Constantius, thereby exiling Athanasius. This time Athanasius hid out in the suburbs of Alexandria. Four months passed during which the masses of the people kept rioting in favor of their archbishop, forcing Valens to restore Athanasius to his see. The bishop served safely in his see for the last eight years of his life.

3 ✛ Sts. Timothy and Maura

Place: Upper Thebes, Egypt
Fame: Newlywed martyrs

The young couple Timothy and Maura (d.c. 298) had been married only twenty days when the anti-Christian edict of

Emperor Diocletian (r. 284–305) was applied to them in a most cruel fashion.

Timothy was serving as a lector in the church at Penapeis near Antinoe. When he refused to hand over to the pagan governor the church's sacred texts, his persecutors tortured him. They poked a red-hot iron rod inside his ears and cut off his eyelids. Timothy, however, remained steadfast in his faith. The authorities then sent for his recent bride so that she might persuade him to recant his faith and relinquish the books. When Maura arrived, instead of urging her husband to yield the texts and save his life, she whispered to him to remain strong and save his soul. Immediately, Maura too was seized. The soldiers brutally ripped out her hair from her head. The persecutors then nailed the couple to a wall, where they lingered dying for nine days.

9 ✠ St. Pachomius

Place: Upper Thebes, Egypt
Fame: Founder of the communal monastic life

Pachomius (c. 292–348) converted from the pagan religion of his parents to Christianity after he experienced at Latopolis the kindness of Christians toward him and other newly conscripted Roman army recruits as they were being transported roughly down the Nile River. Upon discharge from the army, Pachomius returned to his home at Khenoboskion, where he became a catechumen and received baptism in 313.

Wanting to give himself fully to the grace of conversion, he searched in the desert for the hermit Palemon, who was renowned for holiness. About 320, when Pachomius was visiting at Tabennisi on the east bank of the Nile, just north of Thebes, he received an inspiration to organize into a community the numerous individual disciples who were flocking to him. "He was the first — not, indeed, to gather round him communities of Christian ascetics on a large scale — but to organize them and draw up in writing a rule for their common use."[3] Among Pachomius's first recruits were his brother and sister. The brother joined Pachomius's male community. The sister entered the women's community, which took up quarters in the convent that Pachomius had built for them directly across the Nile from his monastery.

His rule required obedience to superiors, common ownership of goods, shared profits from labor, rote memorization of the Scriptures, modesty of the eyes, silence at table, assisting at Mass on Saturdays and Sundays, and communal recitation of the psalms in the morning, evening, and night. The genius of his rule was the individual application and mitigation it permitted according to each monk's abilities and desires for prayer, penance, fasting, and practical labor. Pachomius's intention was to provide communal support for the demanding monastic life.

Because he spoke openly and often against the popular heresy of Arianism, he was denounced by an opponent as a heretic to the episcopal council at Latopolis. After an investigation, he was acquitted of all charges. Athanasius, the preeminent opponent of Arianism, visited Pachomius in 333 to thank him for, and to encourage him in, his fidelity to the teachings of the Church.

At the time of his death, after a quarter century of his having welcomed monks, it is estimated that over three thousand men and women had come to live in the nine monasteries for men and two convents for women that he had founded. He neither was ordained nor did he permit his monks to be ordained. His rule, written only after decades of experience, served as the archetypal rule for the next three centuries for monks in Africa, the Middle East, and western Europe. "Although St. Antony is often considered the founder of Christian monasticism, that title belongs more properly to St. Pachomius."[4] Pachomius had initiated the idea and implemented the transition from the solitary eremetical life to communal cenobitical monasticism.

15 ✢ St. Isidore of Chios

Place: *Alexandria, Egypt*
Fame: *Soldier-martyr*

The story is told that Isidore (d. 251) worked as a military officer in charge of the commissary in the army of Emperor Diocletian (r. 284–305). He was assigned to leave his native Alexandria and sail under the command of Numerius to the Aegean island of Chios.

During the journey, Isidore's captain discovered that this Roman soldier was a Christian. "Placed on trial, he showed great constancy, threats and promises proving equally unavailing. As he refused to sacrifice, his tongue was cut out and he was beheaded. His body was sunk in a well, but it was recovered by the Christians."[5] Two Christians are credited with giving Isidore's body proper burial: the soldier Ammianus and the woman Myrope. Eventually both of these rescuers were martyred: Ammianus at Cyzicus for professing the Christian faith; Myrope for her retrieving and burying the bodies of many martyrs.

Miracles allegedly occurred at the well into which Isidore's body has been dumped. A basilica was built over the tomb of Isidore. Although the cult of Isidore spread in less than three centuries from Africa to Constantinople, Russia, and France, the historical character of the story is doubted.

22 ✝ St. Julia of Carthage and Corsica

Place: *Carthage (now in Tunisia)*
Fame: *Enslaved to a Syrian merchant, martyred at Corsica*

The account of the life of Julia (sixth century) is based admittedly "on a late tradition and has been freely embellished with imaginative detail."[6] Her name, nonetheless, is recorded in Church history on the lists of the most significant martyrs. Scholars claim that she was a historical figure, but that her story needs to be modified to her having been martyred not by a Corsican governor but probably by Saracen pirates.

The original story asserts that Julia was captured during the Vandal invasion of Carthage in 439. She was sold as a slave to a Syrian merchant named Eusebius, who allowed her to continue to practice the Christian faith. When Eusebius sailed from Syria to Gaul, he took along his trusted servant. The ship docked at Corsica, at the northern port that is known today as Cape Corso. Eusebius debarked to participate in a local heathen festival, but Julia remained on board in order to avoid celebrating the feast of a false god. Although the governor implored Eusebius to order Julia to join in the celebration, he refused because of his respect for her and the services she rendered to him. Later that night, however, after Eusebius had collapsed asleep in a drunken stupor, the governor ordered Julia to be brought ashore. Standing in front of the governor, Julia refused to sacrifice to the gods despite the offer of freeing her from enslavement. Julia held her ground. The governor ordered her to be beaten and crucified.

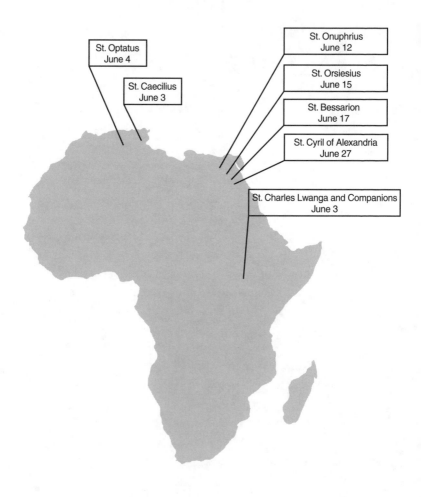

Ven. Pierre Toussaint
June 30
Haiti and USA

St. Onuphrius
June 12

St. Optatus
June 4

St. Orsiesius
June 15

St. Caecilius
June 3

St. Bessarion
June 17

St. Cyril of Alexandria
June 27

St. Charles Lwanga and Companions
June 3

JUNE

〜∾

3 ✢ St. Charles Lwanga and Companions

Place: Namugongo, Buganda (now in Uganda)
Fame: Suffered martyrdom rather than
succumb to sexual advances

In Uganda, which declared its independence in 1962 and took
its name from the province Buganda, Christianity had been
introduced in 1879 by Catholic missionaries. King Mutesa was
receptive to the religion. His successor, Mwanga, however, was
not. Besides having murdered a Protestant missionary and his
entourage, Mwanga repeatedly practiced pedophilia with the
royal pages. When the Christian steward of the pages, Joseph
Mukasa, dared to reprimand the king for his immoral behavior,
Mwanga instituted an anti-Christian persecution. Mwanga decreed that Joseph Mukasa would be his first victim and that he
should be burned alive. The executioner, however, had mercy
on the young man and beheaded him before burning the body.
On the evening of the death of Joseph Mukasa, November 15,
1885, Charles Lwanga requested and received baptism.

About six months later, a new wave of anti-Christian slaughter was initiated. On May 25, 1886, the king discovered that the
fourteen-year-old page Muwafu had been receiving instructions in the Christian faith from an older page, Denis
Sebuggwawo. The king grew furious. He ordered the instructor to be brought before him. Mwanga confronted Denis, who
admitted his role as religious instructor. The king thrust a spear
through the neck of the youth and ordered an assistant to kill
him. "That night the king gave orders for the death of every

Christian in the royal enclosure, Catholic or not; precautions were taken to prevent their escape, and executioners were summoned."[1] That night, Charles Lwanga, who had succeeded Joseph Mukasa as master of the pages, led an all-night vigil for the Christians, both the baptized and catechumens. Charles himself baptized four boys that night. In the morning, the king ordered all the pages to report to him.

At the king's court, Mwanga told the assembled young men: "Those of you who do not pray, stand by me. Those who pray [that is, who are Christians], go over there."[2] Nineteen young men and boys stood across from the king. He then asked if it was true that they were Christians. The group answered affirmatively. The king replied, "Then you shall all be burnt! Away with you, and eat your cow in your Father's house in Heaven!"[3] The phrase "eat your cow" refers to enjoying a great feast. The group of nineteen, bound in ropes and chains, was led away. They were force-marched overnight thirty-seven miles from the king's residence at Munyonyo to the place of execution at Namugongo. At their destination they were jailed for a week.

A huge funeral pyre was prepared, but was not yet set aflame. Each of the boys was laid upon a mat, bound, and placed onto the pyre. One boy, Mbaga, was the son of the chief executioner who twice had encouraged his son to run away and hide, but Mbaga refused. The father then asked one of the guards to kill the boy with a blow on the neck to save him the torturous pain of the fire. All were burned on the pyre, except Charles Lwanga, who was kept apart for special torture by slow burning on a separate pyre.

Other martyrs counted in this group of twenty-two include Andrew Kagwa, who was the Catholic chief of Kigowa and had converted the sons of the king's counselor; and the Catholic district judge at Mityana, Matthias Kalemba. Others were Joseph Mukasa, Denis Ssebuggwawo, Pontian Ngondwe, Athanasius Bazzekuketta, Mbaga Tuzinde, Gonzaga Gonza, Noah Mawaggali, John Mary Muzeyi, Luke Banabakintu, James Buzabaliawo, Bruno Serunkuma, Mugagga, Kizito, Muskasa Kiriwawanvu, Gyavira, Adolph Ludigo, Anatole Kiriggwajjo, Ambrose Kibuka, and Achilles Kiwanuka.

While an exact number is impossible to ascertain, it seems that approximately twenty-three Protestant martyrs also were killed similarly by King Mwanga.[4]

3 ✞ St. Caecilius

Place: Carthage (now in Tunisia)
Fame: Spiritual father of the great St. Cyprian

Caecilius (d.c. 248), whose name sometimes is rendered as Caecilianus, is reputed to have been the elderly priest whose example and instruction inspired and guided St. Cyprian in his conversion from paganism to Christianity.

Cyprian seems to have lived for some years in Caecilius's home. The future bishop, martyr, as well as Father and Doctor of the Church refers to Caecilius as "the father of his new life."[5] When Caecilius was dying, he entrusted his wife and children to the care of Cyprian.

4 ✞ St. Optatus

Place: Milevis, Numidia (now in Algeria)
Fame: Outstanding opponent of Donatism

Optatus (d.c. 387), the bishop of Milevis, was considered among the most important bishops of the African Church. He was ranked by St. Fulgentius, the famous sixth-century Carthaginian bishop, on a par with St. Augustine and St. Ambrose because of Optatus's doctrinal defense of the faith. St. Augustine described Optatus as similar to St. Cyprian of Carthage and St. Hilary of Poitiers in that all three saintly bishops had converted from paganism to Christianity.

In approximately 370, Optatus entered wholeheartedly into the Donatist controversy. Donatism literally was dividing the Church by establishing competing structures of bishoprics and clergy and declaring that the Donatists and not the Catholics were the true Church of Jesus Christ. Optatus's treatise, *Against Parmenian the Donatist,* was the first attempt to refute Donatism and its protagonist Parmenius, the bishop of Carthage. The original work, which Optatus revised fifteen years later, remains extant. "It is a historically important document, since in it he (Optatus) speaks of the supremacy of the pope, the validity of the sacraments, and refers to the veneration of relics."[6]

Optatus demonstrated a clear preference for conciliation rather than confrontation. Because he wanted to win back the Donatists to the Catholic Church, he described the Donatists as schismatics rather than heretics. Using a historical and doctrinal methodology, Optatus demonstrated that the Catholic Church, and not the Donatists, enjoyed constant succession with the chair of Peter at Rome. The pastoral bishop of Milevis urged the Donatists not to rebaptize lapsed Christians, since the validity of the sacraments depended on Christ, who is the originator of the sacraments, and not on the individual priest, who acts as Christ's agent in conferring the sacrament. When critics chastised the peacemaker Optatus for having fomented persecution against the Donatists, he refused to accept responsibility for the violent action, since the civil power, and not Church authorities, had initiated and conducted the police action against the Donatists.

12 ✛ St. Onuphrius

Place: Thebaid, Egypt
Fame: A hermit for seventy years

St. Paphnutius related the following story about his vocation. He went into the desert region of the Thebaid to discern if he possessed a vocation to the eremetical life. Midway through the third week of his retreat, Paphnutius encountered a very old man with long hair and a beard, dressed only in a loincloth made of leaves. The young man began to walk away hurriedly from this strange character. The old man shouted to the pass-erby, however, and invited him to chat. The old man was Onuphrius (d.c. 400).

The two men spent that afternoon, overnight, and the next morning together. They talked about the spiritual life and its demands, with Paphnutius asking the questions and Onuphrius supplying responses. Onuphrius informed Paphnutius that he had lived in the desert for seventy years. He had begun his desert life as a member of a monastery, but after a while discovered that he preferred to live alone as a hermit. In the desert he had suffered much from privation of food and drink, and from many temptations. That evening at sunset, the pair shared a meal of bread and water. All night long, they prayed together.

In the morning, Paphnutius noticed that Onuphrius seemed to be quite ill. The younger asked the elder if he needed some assistance. Onuphrius responded that, providentially, God had sent Paphnutius to Onuphrius to bury him. With that having been said, Onuphrius died.

Paphnutius tore his tunic in half, wrapped it around the old man, and buried the body in a crevice of the mountain wall near the entrance to the old man's cave. For a few moments, Paphnutius himself considered using the now vacant cave, when suddenly the roof collapsed, and his question was answered unequivocably. Paphnutius then made himself a disciple of the great St. Antony.

15 ✠ St. Orsiesius

Place: Upper Thebaid, Egypt
Fame: Abbot

The famous St. Pachomius hand-picked two promising aspirants, Orsiesius (d.c. 380) and Theodore, to receive his personal formation in the monastic life. The master made this pair of disciples his traveling companions on visitations and his consultants on writing the common rule.

Despite his youth, Orsiesius was appointed abbot of various monasteries. His leadership, however, was not always appreciated by the older monks. At Khenoboski, the older monks murmured against their newly appointed leader, wondering how someone so young could presume to guide the more experienced senior monks. Pachomius defended the appointment by asking rhetorically, "Is the kingdom of God only for the elderly?"[7] At Tabennisi, Orsiesius was elected abbot when the master Pachomius died and his immediate successor, Petronius, lived just thirteen days more than the master. At first, the monks in Pachomius's foundation happily received their master's young disciple. After a few years, however, the monks complained increasingly about their superior. They felt he enforced too strictly the common rules regarding use and ownership of property. After enduring many complaints and not wishing to be the occasion for division within the monastery, Orsiesius stepped down from his position as superior. Orsiesius' original co-disciple, Theodore, was elected. Not wishing to cause affront to his esteemed companion, Theodore, in all his decisions, conferred with Orsiesius and even appointed him co-visitor to the local monasteries. When Theodore died in 368, Orsiesius again was appointed abbot, which position he held until his death a dozen years later.

Antony and Athanasius, the two highly revered saints, wrote in praise of Orsiesius' life and selection as superior of the monastery at Tabennisi.

17 ✚ St. Bessarion

Place: Deserts of Nitria and Skete, Egypt
Fame: Miracle worker

The Egyptian Bessarion (d. fourth century) chose to live his Christian life wandering in the desert in an area bordered on the east by the Red Sea and on the west by the deserts at Skete and Nitria. In the east, Bessarion first made himself a disciple of St. Antony and later St. Macarius. In the west, he met St. John Cassian and St. Pambo. "We are told that rather than live under a roof he wandered about like a bird, observing silence and subduing his flesh by extreme fasting. He is said to have once gone forty days without food, standing in prayer amid brambles."[8] Many miracles are attributed to him: walking on the Nile, making salt water fresh, making rain fall in the midst of a drought, and many other marvelous deeds. Extraordinary austerities regarding food, clothing, and shelter are attributed to him.

27 ✚ St. Cyril of Alexandria

Place: Alexandria, Egypt
Fame: Father and Doctor of the Church

Cyril (d. 444) was born, raised, and educated at the cosmopolitan capital city of Alexandria. His uncle, Patriarch Theophilus of Alexandria, ordained Cyril a priest and, in 403, took the young cleric to Constantinople to attend what later became known as the infamous Synod of the Oak, which condemned and deposed St. John Chrysostom. Nine years later, when Theophilus died, Cyril succeeded his uncle as patriarch. The nephew's disposition reflected the uncle's manner: "He revealed affinities to his impetuous, high-handed uncle, especially in the early years of his episcopate."[9] Confrontation marked the first part of his episcopate (412–429); conciliation more often characterized the latter part (430–444).

Cyril challenged a seemingly endless stream of opponents. In his writings against Julian the Apostate, Cyril criticized the pagans and their beliefs. He attempted to have the Jews expelled from the capital city because of their physical and verbal attacks against Christians and because of Jewish efforts to convert Christians. He antagonized the local Roman governor Orestes by honoring the monk Ammonius, who had physically and verbally attacked Orestes. Cyril himself allegedly incited a riot against the learned Neoplatonist philosopher Hypatia, whom a Christian mob later dragged from her carriage and literally tore her to pieces.

Against fellow Christians, however, Cyril unleashed his harshest attacks. Cyril refused to include the name of the heroic martyr John Chrysostom on the Church's list of saints. Chrysostom had been condemned falsely in 403 at the Synod of the Oak. To eliminate the influence of the heretical Novatians, Cyril confiscated their property and closed their churches. Against the heretical Arians, he devoted a decade of vitriolic writing until 428. When the heretic Nestorius became patriarch of Constantinople in 428, Cyril criticized his former fellow patriarch until Cyril himself died. At the ecumenical Council of Ephesus in 431, Cyril introduced and concluded in one day the hearings that ended in the condemnation of Nestorius. These proceedings took place four or five days before approximately four dozen bishops from Antioch and other Eastern sees arrived to explain and defend Nestorius and his teachings.

The latter part of Cyril's years as bishop were marked by reconciliation. He learned to listen to the ideas behind the language that was separating him and his opponents. In 433, he signed the Symbol of Union, whereby he yielded his prior insistence on certain phrases that he favored and accepted the language and concepts preferred by others. He even admitted and explained that while his own teachings sounded very much like the previously condemned heresy of Apollinarianism, he differed from and did not support that false teaching. He accepted limits also on his understanding of the Blessed Virgin Mary's title of *Theotokos*. During the events of 433, Cyril was vindicated, but he was humbled too. "Cyril's reaction to the Symbol of Union reveals a remarkable maturing on his part."[10] From this time forward, extremists on both sides pushed Cyril to abandon his position of compromise. On the one hand, some allies thought he had abandoned their anti-Nestorian position by not condemning Nestorius's teacher Theodore of Mopsuestia. On the other hand, some enemies refused to reconcile with Cyril because they remembered that he had condemned Nestorius.

While he wrote on a wide range of exegetical and theological topics, "Cyril's claim to theological immortality rests on his role in the development of Christology."[11] His prolific writings can be divided into two periods: up to 428, generally against the Arians, and after 428, generally against the Nestorians.

30 ✠ Ven. Pierre Toussaint

Place: New York City, United States of America
Fame: Lay leader, exemplary churchman

Pierre Toussaint (d. 1853) was born a slave in Haiti and died a freeman in New York City. (Conflicting records show that he could have been born anytime between 1766 and 1778.) He lived his Catholic faith so well that he gained in his lifetime the reputation of sanctity. On December 17, 1996, his name passed the first of three stages in the process of being declared officially a saint in the Roman Catholic Church.

Pierre grew up as a third-generation domestic slave in the household of French colonists named Berard. Pierre was taught to read and write and to play the violin in order to tutor the children of his master. He was instructed in etiquette and the ways of the wealthy.

In the midst of slave revolts in Haiti, the Berard family fled to New York City. The spirit of fighting for equality that had ignited the French Revolution in 1789 made its way to this Caribbean island also. Slave owners and slave rebels both committed atrocities.

Pierre, along with his sister, arrived on August 21, 1797, in New York City. He continued as the family's servant. Because the leaders of the slave revolts had invited the plantation owners to return in order to jump-start the stalled economy, Jean Berard traveled to Haiti in 1801. He had hoped to return to his estate, but discovered that all his property was "irretrievably lost."[12] Before being able to return to New York, he contracted pleurisy and died.

Young Marie Berard was awaiting her husband's return to New York. She was heartbroken when she received the news. She tried to run the household, but she ran into debt instead.

She was a woman of leisure; she had no marketable skills. Her brother moved into the home, but while he was an excellent musician, he too could not earn a sufficient living. Ironically, Pierre provided a living for the entire family. He had been trained in New York City, at the suggestion of Mrs. Berard, as a hairdresser. Pierre possessed great skill and ease in dealing with all women of wealth. Among his clients were the granddaughters of the Revolutionary War heroes Alexander Hamilton and Gen. Philip Schuyler. Young Ms. Schuyler preserved many letters and documents relevant to Pierre's life. She refers affectionately to Pierre as "my saint." She was not Catholic, but she knew she was dealing with an extraordinary person. Her records are housed in the New York City Public Library.

Marie Berard wanted to emancipate Pierre. The signs of the times called for the abolition of slavery. Also, she was unable to provide for his living. Pierre, however, refused emancipation. The family was providing him with a home and he was happy to provide a living for them. A few days before Mrs. Berard died of tuberculosis in 1807, she and Pierre signed an agreement directing that he be emancipated upon her death.

Pierre married Juliette Gaston in 1811. They were not able to conceive. They adopted his dying sister's daughter when she was six months old. Pierre and Juliette cared for her until she died at fourteen years of age. Just before his wife died, Pierre and Juliette had celebrated forty years of marriage.

Pierre practiced his Catholic faith in exemplary fashion. He attended daily Mass in New York City's only Catholic church, which was St. Peter's on Barclay Street in Lower Manhattan. He assisted St. Elizabeth Ann Seton in her home at Battery Park in raising funds for orphaned children, which work he supported for four decades. He began the city's first school for black children. He helped to provide funds for the Oblate Sisters of Providence, which was a religious community of black nuns founded in Baltimore. He made food, clothing, and shelter available to fellow black refugees from Haiti. He ministered to the sick and dying during a yellow fever epidemic when many of the city's political leaders fled the city in search of healthier rural climates. He was proud to be black — and he was proud to be Catholic.

On at least two occasions, Pierre suffered the humiliation of racism. Once, this pillar of the parish church was asked by an ignorant usher to leave the church because Pierre was black. Pierre, who was seventy-six years old at the time, was a leader among the faithful in depth of faith, in expressing charity, in evangelization, and in assisting anyone in need regardless of one's religion and race. After the usher escorted him out of the church, Pierre absorbed the hurt in emulation of his master, Jesus Christ, that is, without a word of complaint. On a second occasion, a friend suggested to the elderly and arthritic Pierre that he return home by way of a horse-drawn carriage. Pierre responded that he was not able to ride in a carriage because of his skin color. He then walked home.

Soon after Pierre died in 1853, those who knew him suggested that he be considered for public recognition among the saints of the Church. His remains were removed to St. Patrick's Cathedral in Lower Manhattan. In 1990, his remains were transferred to the new St. Patrick's Cathedral in midtown Manhattan. He is the only lay person buried there. His vault lies alongside those of the cardinal-archbishops of New York City.

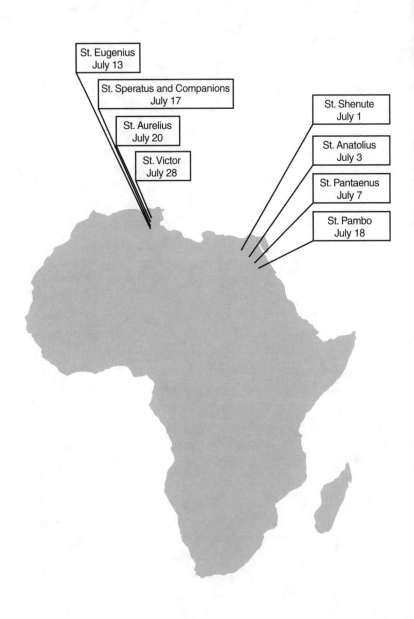

JULY

1 ✢ St. Shenute

Place: *Thebes, Egypt*
Fame: *Promoter of moderation in the monastic life*

Born and raised at Shenalolet in Egypt, Shenute (c. 332–c. 450) moved to the Dair-al-Abiad monastery near Atripe in the Thebaid in approximately 380, when he was about forty-eight years old. Five years later, upon the death of the abbot, who was his uncle, Shenute was named the successor.

Shenute ruled with an iron fist. He imposed upon the members a strict rule of moral and monastic living: no lying, cheating, or stealing, and maintaining silence as well as the practice of service, prayer, and chaste living. Transgressions met with swift and stern penalties. Despite the rigid rule, disciples flocked to the monastery. Shenute's biographer Besa reports that twenty-two hundred monks and eighteen hundred nuns lived at one time under Shenute's leadership. Two innovations attributed to Shenute include a stricter version of the rule introduced by Pachomius and a vow formula to which all disciples committed themselves. Lest an unfair image of Shenute be portrayed, it must be remembered that almost all of his subjects were illiterate farmers and that the monks typically competed to perform the most severe penances, fasts, and false mysticism. The way that Shenute managed to moderate these excessive practices was to maintain legitimately strict control over his disciples.

Like St. Antony and St. Pachomius, Shenute is regarded as one of the outstanding figures in the monastic world of the fourth and fifth centuries in Egypt. He became the head of all the other abbots in the area. Just as monks of a particular monastery recognized the authority of their particular abbot, so too the abbots of the general area recognized the general authority of Shenute.

Some scholars suggest that Shenute accompanied St. Cyril of Alexandria to the ecumenical Council of Ephesus in 431. Shenute, who is regarded as "the only prominent original writer in Coptic," wrote numerous sermons and letters of spiritual direction.[1]

3 ✛ St. Anatolius

Place: Alexandria, Egypt
Fame: Political prelate

During the rancorous and tumultuous period following St. Flavian's brutal death at the infamous Robber Synod, Anatolius was elected to fill the saint's local episcopal see at Constantinople. Anatolius was blessed with much courage. At the Council of Ephesus, he had opposed publicly the teachings of the popular Nestorius. Now, almost twenty years later, he was willing to serve in a see riddled by strife, division, and death. Anatolius, a native of Alexandria, compounded his difficulties by having asked to be ordained bishop of Constantinople by Dioscorus, the archbishop of Alexandria.

The new bishop of Constantinople convened a council there to promote acceptance of Pope St. Leo's famous letter generally known as "the Tome," which had aroused the enemies who then killed Flavian. In the face of opposition, Anatolius publicly declared his acceptance of the letter and required each of his metropolitan bishops to do the same. The letter included an unequivocal condemnation of Nestorius and Euthyches. Having achieved strong episcopal support for orthodoxy, Anatolius wrote a letter to the pope requesting that the Holy Father might officially recognize Anatolius as the legitimate successor to Flavian. The pope, however, haltingly accepted Anatolius's election because the bishop had allowed himself to be ordained by Bishop Dioscorus, a heretical Monophysite.

One year later, in 451, the pope convened the great Council of Chalcedon. This ecumenical council declared the faith of the Church regarding its understanding of Jesus and Mary, and repeated previous condemnations of Nestorianism and Monophysitism. Because Anatolius played a prominent role in achieving the results desired by the pope, Anatolius's influence became second only to the papal legates themselves. Unfortunately, at the fifteenth and final session of the council, from which the papal legates were absent, the Eastern bishops, led by Anatolius, declared that Constantinople was second in authority only to Rome. This declaration rejected the traditional places of authority possessed by the more ancient churches of Alexandria and Antioch. This time the pope did not accept the result of Anatolius's maneuvering but rejected outright the Egyptian's proposed conciliar canon. The pope reprimanded Anatolius for his machinations, saying that "a Catholic, especially if he be a priest of the Lord, should not be corrupted by ambition any more than involved in error."[2]

7 ✚ St. Pantaenus

Place: Alexandria, Egypt
Fame: Head of the catechetical school at Alexandria

Pantaenus (c. 140-c. 200) is remembered for having improved significantly the reputation of the Alexandrian catechetical school that he headed in approximately 180. Little else is known about this great educator. None of his works is extant. Some reputable sources claim that he may have been born at Sicily rather than Alexandria.[3]

One of Pantaenus's students, St. Clement of Alexandria, wrote glowingly of his teacher. The historian Eusebius describes Pantaenus as a man of "great learning, ardent and zealous in the preaching of the word."[4] St. Jerome reported that Pantaenus was a missionary, perhaps either to India, Southern Arabia, Yemen, or Ethiopia. It seems that the people to whom he ministered had already received St. Matthew's Gospel from the apostle St. Bartholomew.

13 ✛ St. Eugenius

Place: *Carthage (now in Tunisia)*
Fame: *Defender of religious freedom*

For over a hundred years, from 429 to 534, the barbarian Vandals ruled what previously had been the Western Roman Empire's stronghold in Africa. The Vandals invaded Mauretania in 429 and soon settled along the coastal provinces of Mauretania Tingitana, Mauretania Caesaria, and Numidia, before seizing and establishing in 439 at Carthage an independent kingdom, from which base they attacked and sacked Rome in 455. These Arian Vandals, from time to time, persecuted the Catholic Christians. Among the six successive Vandal kings, the worst persecutors were Genseric (r. 428–477), his son Huneric (r. 477–484), and Thrasimund (r. 496–523). Eugenius (d. 505) lived and suffered during the reigns of the last two named kings.

The episcopal see of Carthage had been vacant for over half a century when Huneric relented temporarily in 481 from his intolerance of Catholicism and invited the Catholics to elect a bishop. The people overwhelmingly chose Eugenius, who enjoyed a reputation for scholarship and service. Assuming his position, he went about doing good, praying with the people, and dispensing generously from the few material goods that he possessed. Huneric grew uncomfortable with Eugenius's increasing popularity among the people. The king called in the bishop to discuss the matter. The king unilaterally forbade the bishop either to preach publicly or to allow Vandals to enter the Catholic churches. The bishop replied that he would refuse to close the church doors to anybody who wished to enter the church. The king then stationed at the churches' doors numerous guards who stopped from entering those whose external appearance in dress or hairstyle indicated that they might be Vandals. The soldiers brutally mistreated many persons who were trying to enter the church. The soldiers "used forked sticks which, twisted into the hair and violently drawn back, tore off hair and skin together. Some thus lost their eyes, others died, and women who had been scalped in this way were led through the streets as a warning to others. A fierce persecution was thus initiated."[5]

In an attempt to create political unity through religious conformity, Huneric convened a Church council at Carthage in 484. Because the Arians far outnumbered the Catholics, Eugenius challenged in the council the validity of whatever the council might decide. Huneric abruptly ended the proceedings by encircling the Catholic bishops, robbing them and their entourages, and exiling them. Eugenius was sent to Tripoli, where an Arian bishop mistreated him. Along the way, Eugenius managed to send a letter to his congregation back in the capital city. He wrote: "I with tears beg, exhort and implore you, by the dreadful day of judgment and the awful light of the coming of Christ, that you hold fast the Catholic faith. Keep the grace of baptism and the anointing of chrism. Let no man born again of water return to the water."[6] Eugenius was exhorting the faithful not to undergo rebaptism, which the Arians required.

The vicissitudes of tolerance and intolerance continued after

Huneric's death in 484. Huneric's nephew Gontamund (r. 484-496) gradually reversed his uncle's anti-Catholic policies. In 488, Bishop Eugenius and other clergy were recalled from exile, and over the course of the next few years, churches were recovered from the Arians, restored to the Catholics, and reopened. This respite ceased when Thrasimund (r. 496-523) ascended the throne. He condemned Eugenius to death, but then commuted the sentence to lifelong exile. Eugenius was sent to Languedoc, in southeast Gaul, where he died in the monastery at Albi.

17 ✟ St. Speratus and Companions

Place: Scillium (now in Tunisia)
Fame: First recorded Christian martyrs in Africa

Marcus Aurelius (r. 161-180), the philosopher-emperor, ordered an empire-wide persecution of Christians in 174. Even though the emperor had died on March 17, 180, governors continued to enforce the imperial demand. Four months later, on July 17, local pagan citizens informed soldiers of the names of a dozen Christians: seven men (Speratus, Nartzalus, Cittinus, Veturius, Felix, Aquilinus, and Laetantius) and five women (Januaria, Generosa, Vestia, Donata, and Secunda). This happened at Scillium, near Carthage. The group of a dozen martyrs is known also as the Scillitan Martyrs.

Speratus and his companions were led by soldiers to the court of the Roman proconsul Publius Vigellius Saturninus at Carthage. The Roman official offered clemency to the Christians if they would pray publicly before the Roman gods. Speratus, acting as spokesperson for the group, responded: "We have never committed any crime, we have injured no one; we have given thanks for the evil treatment we have received because we hold our sovereign in honor."

The official said, "We also are religious people, and more-over our religion is simple. We swear by the divine spirit of our lord the emperor and pray for his safety."[7] Speratus attempted to explain the Christian understanding of true simplicity, but the proconsul interrupted him.

"Their *acta* (the martyrs' deeds), indubitably authentic, are the earliest in existence for the Church in Africa and have suffered little from later editorial 'improvement.'"[8] The following dialogue took place.

Saturninus: I will not listen to anything against our sacred rites. Rather is it for you to swear by our master the emperor's *genius*.

Speratus: I do not recognize an empire of this world. Rather do I serve the God whom no man has seen, whom no man is able to see. I have not stolen, and if I engage in trade I pay the duties, because I recognize my master, the King of kings and ruler of all peoples.

Saturninus   *(to the others)*: Give up these beliefs.

Speratus: That we should do murder or bear false witness, that is the evil belief.

Saturninus: Do not share this lunacy.

Cittinus: We have no one to fear except the Lord our God who is in Heaven.

Donata: We give to Caesar the honour that is due to Caesar, but we fear God alone.

Vestia: I am a Christian.

Secunda: So am I, and I want to be nothing else.

Saturninus   *(to Speratus)*: Are you still resolved to remain a Christian? [Speratus replied that he was, and all the other prisoners agreed.]

Saturninus: "Will you take time to think about it?"

Speratus:	There is nothing to think about when what is right is so clear.
Saturninus:	What have you got in your case?
Speratus:	The Books, and the letters of a righteous man called Paul.
Saturninus:	I offer you a remand of thirty days, to reconsider the matter.

The twelve insisted that more time would not alter their faith. They reaffirmed that they were Christians. Saturninus then imposed the death sentence. As he read aloud each person's name, each victim proclaimed aloud, "Thanks be to God."[9] Nartzalus added, "This day we are martyrs in Heaven."[10]

18 ✛ St. Pambo

Place: Nitrian desert, Egypt
Fame: Co-worker with and counselor for saints

After Pambo (d.c. 390) was inspired and educated in the monastic life by St. Antony of the Desert, Pambo, in turn, inspired other monks and holy persons. At his monastery in the Nitrian desert on the outskirts of Alexandria, he instructed fellow monks Sts. Dioscorus, Ammon, Eusebius, and Euthymius and worked alongside in the same community with the famous St. Isidore of Pelusium, St. Macarius the Elder, and St. Macarius the Younger. Many people, including St. Athanasius of Alexandria, St. Melania the Elder of Rome, and Rufinus, came to the desert to visit with, learn from, and receive advice from Pambo.

Contemporaries describe Pambo as especially reflective at prayer, brief in his comments, and tactless. On Pambo's first day with his instructor, his teacher suggested that Pambo pray over Psalm 39 (or 38, in earlier versions of the Bible). The teacher read the psalm's first line, after which Pambo interrupted the teacher and took leave of him. The line was: "I will take heed of my ways that I sin not with my tongue." Having reflected on the one line, Pambo returned to his teacher six months later. Another story reports that the wealthy Roman widow Melania visited Pambo and donated to the poor monk three hundred pounds of silver. He never said a word of thanks. He simply responded by saying that he would distribute the money to the poorest monasteries. She pointed out to him that the gift was especially large. He shot back, "He to whom you offered this gift has no need for you to tell Him its value."[11] Another person made a donation and asked the holy man to count the sum of money. Abruptly again, Pambo retorted: "God does not ask how much, but how."[12]

Pambo lived the monk's life in exemplary fashion. He ate and dressed simply. He prayed for long hours at a time. He earned his keep by weaving palm frond mats. On his deathbed, he confided to Melania, who was assisting him, "Since I came into the desert, I have eaten nothing that I have not earned by work, and I do not remember that I have ever said anything for which I had need to be sorry afterwards. Nevertheless, I must now go to God before I have even begun to serve Him."[13]

20 ✢ St. Aurelius

Place: Carthage (now in Tunisia)
Fame: Active respondent to contemporary heresies

About 392, Aurelius (d. 430) was ordained bishop of Carthage. "At this time the great church of northern Africa was at the height of its power and influence, and the bishop of Carthage, being in effect its primate, was one of the most important of all Christian prelates."[14]

At this same time, the heresies of Donatism and Pelagianism were prevalent among the clergy and laity. Donatism was losing popularity, but Pelagianism was gaining strength. Aurelius wasted no time in responding to the errors of both teachings. He convened numerous provincial and regional synods to deal with these theological issues. He also called for greater popular participation in the liturgy and introduced into the celebration of Mass the singing of the psalms.

A contemporary of Aurelius was St. Augustine of Hippo. The two met for the first time in 388, when Augustine stopped at Carthage on his way home from Italy. When Aurelius was being ordained bishop of Carthage in 396, Augustine at nearby Hippo was celebrating his first anniversary of priesthood and four years later was himself named bishop. For the next thirty years, these two bishops collaborated in many Church issues. Together they confronted with written and spoken words the teachings and tactics of prominent heretics. When Aurelius complained to Augustine about the apparent laziness of monks under the guise of prayerfulness, Augustine responded by writing his critical essay, "On the Work of Monks." Augustine comments in his *City of God* how he was struck by Aurelius's love of the poor and respect for the truths of the Christian religion.[15] These two friends died just a couple of weeks apart, with Aurelius preceding Augustine.

28 ✠ St. Victor

Place: Probably Carthage (now in Tunisia)
Fame: Pope from 189 to 199

Victor (d.c. 199) was the first pope whose cultural background was Latin rather than Greek. Until his election in 189, all previous thirteen popes had come from the eastern part of the Roman Empire. Because he promoted the use of the Latin language, culture, and traditions, the Church in his time shifted its orientation from Greek to Latin. He was also the first pope from Africa.

The most significant issue with which Victor dealt was determining a universal date for the celebration of Easter. He convened synods throughout the Christian world, from the provinces of western Gaul to eastern Mesopotamia. He posed to the bishops the question whether the celebration of Easter ought to be restricted to Sunday only, or to be celebrated on any day of the week. Until then, the Church's practice in the West was to regard every Sunday as a memorial of Jesus' resurrection, but without having established any particular Sunday as an annual Western celebration of the feast of Easter Sunday.

In the East, on the other hand, the Church celebrated Easter on the fourteenth day of the Jewish month of Nissan, that is, the feast of Passover, whether that date fell on a Sunday or not. The fourteenth day is translated in Latin as *quartodeciman*; therefore, the adherents of the Eastern practice were called Quartodecimans. All the Christian world's episcopal synods, except those in Asia Minor led by Polycrates of Ephesus, reported back to Victor that they preferred that Easter be celebrated on a Sunday rather than on the fourteenth day of Nissan. Victor then universally imposed this date.

A storm of protest arose. Bishop Polycrates of Ephesus and

the churches in Asia Minor refused to obey Victor's order. The pope threatened to excommunicate Polycrates and all the Quartodecimans. Even moderate bishops like St. Irenaeus of Lyons, who supported Victor's date for Easter, opposed the pope's harsh treatment of the Quartodecimans. Irenaeus pointed out that the date for celebrating Easter was an unessential discipline rather than an essential doctrine. He added that the Western Church for almost two centuries had not had a special feast for Easter, so why create this controversy over which day of the week to celebrate Easter?

Irenaeus pleaded for moderation and toleration in this matter. He pleaded also for Victor's imitation of all previous popes who had allowed both the East's and West's traditions to flourish simultaneously. The moderate bishops won the day, and the storm subsided. The churches of Asia Minor remained in communion with the Church at Rome and the universal Church. "But the incident itself shows the growing belief of the popes at this time that the Roman church enjoyed some kind of primatial status in the universal Church."[16]

Other incidents, too, arose to force Victor to assert his authority. A leather merchant named Theodotus of Constantinople came to Rome, proclaiming that Jesus was a man blessed with supernatural powers, but only a man and not God. This self-proclaimed prophet taught that the Holy Spirit descended upon Jesus at his baptism as a sign of his having been adopted by God. Victor excommunicated the recalcitrant Theodotus for promoting heretical teachings. At Rome, this pope encountered the priest Florinus who refused to reject Gnostic teachings. Victor deposed the obstinate priest.

Among the many "firsts" attributed to Victor was his successful papal intercession with the imperial household. In order to bring relief to Christians who had been exiled to the salt mines at Sardinia, Victor beseeched Marcia, the Christian common-law wife of the emperor Commodus (r. 180-192). The pope provided the empress with a list of names of Christians whose only crime was their religion. Marcia carried Victor's request to Commodus, who relented and released those identified on the pope's list.

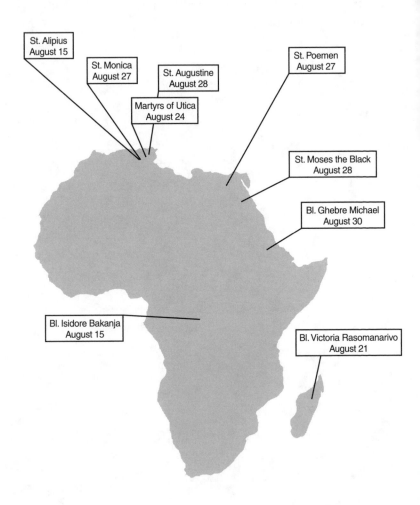

St. Alipius
August 15

St. Monica
August 27

St. Augustine
August 28

Martyrs of Utica
August 24

St. Poemen
August 27

St. Moses the Black
August 28

Bl. Ghebre Michael
August 30

Bl. Isidore Bakanja
August 15

Bl. Victoria Rasomanarivo
August 21

AUGUST

15 ✚ St. Alipius

Place: Tagaste, Numidia (now in Algeria)
Fame: Lifelong friend of St. Augustine of Hippo

The adage "Show me your friends and I'll tell you who you are" applies aptly to Alipius (c. 360-430). He and St. Augustine, who was about six years older than Alipius, were born and raised in the same small town of Tagaste. Their friendship originated as a teacher-student relationship: Augustine taught Alipius grammar at Tagaste and rhetoric at Carthage. At Carthage, Augustine entered the twelve-year heretical Manichaean phase of his life. Alipius fell under this same spell. Alipius's father blamed Augustine for misleading Alipius and forbade his son to have any further contact with his heretical teacher. Separated from Augustine, Alipius sought out other companions. These new friends frequented the circus that consisted in those days of combats between men or between animals, or between men and animals. The contests often deteriorated into blood-soaked bouts. Alipius loved it and lusted after it all. One day, Alipius passed by the area where Augustine was instructing his pupils. The lesson that day focused on the evils of the circus and the weakness of those who delighted in these barbaric behaviors. Unbeknownst to Augustine, Alipius overheard the lecture and decided to change his conduct.

Alipius traveled to Rome, where he devoted himself to the study of law. One day, friends invited him to attend the circus games. When he refused, his friends dragged him forcibly with them. He insisted that he would close his eyes, so that even if he were present physically, he would not be present morally. That strategy worked satisfactorily until the crowd, at one moment, shrieked with horror as one gladiator ferociously stabbed another. Alipius heard the shouts, opened his eyes, and once again opened his heart to these gory games.

After Augustine had left his disinterested students at Carthage in 383 and traveled to Rome in hopes of discovering more serious students, Alipius met with his old friend and renewed their relationship. The next year, when Augustine moved to Milan to accept a teaching position, Alipius moved with him. Augustine began attending the cathedral services because he enjoyed the rhetorical skills of the archbishop St. Ambrose. Eventually, Augustine became so enamored with Ambrose's preaching, not only the style but also the substance, that he decided in September 386 to enter the catechumenate. Alipius joined him in preparing to become a Christian. Retiring to a country house at Cassiciacum, near Milan, the pair devoted themselves, along with Augustine's mother, brother, and son and other devotees to a communal life of prayer, penance, and study. These two friends applied themselves to the process of Christian initiation, and they were baptized together at the Easter Vigil in 387.

The pair returned to Africa in 388. Back at Tagaste, Augustine opened his home to his monastic community, to which Alipius had belonged from its beginning. Three years later, the two friends traveled to Hippo, where they were ordained priests. After a pilgrimage to the Holy Land, Alipius was ordained bishop of his native Tagaste about 393 and Augustine was named bishop of Hippo in 395. For the next three decades, Alipius assisted Augustine in opposing publicly the dying heresy of Manichaeanism and the rising heresies of Donatism and Pelagianism. Both churchmen responded to the social needs created in the wake of the invading Vandal army. Augustine, writing to Alipius in 429, describes his friend as "old."[1] It seems that both men were septuagenarians. The pair had spent their lives searching for truth, discovering Jesus, and serving the Church, while supporting each other in lifelong friendship.

15 ✢ Bl. Isidore Bakanja

Place: *Busira, Congo (now in Zaire)*
Fame: *Young lay martyr*

The young Catholic layman Isidore Bakanja (c. 1885-1909), a member of the Boangi tribe, died for the faith at the hands of a hate-filled atheistic white foreman. The Belgian supervisor Longange had forbidden Isidore either to wear religious symbols or to recite the Rosary while on the job. Isidore, however, who had been educated by the religious brothers of the Cistercian Order of the Strict Observance at Mbandaka, wanted to profess the religion in which he had been baptized just three years previously, and wanted to demonstrate his devotion to the Blessed Virgin Mary of Mount Carmel. At his previous place of employment, Isidore had been permitted by his white supervisor to proselytize among his African co-workers. Isidore, who had made various converts to the faith, wished to continue his evangelizing.

Isidore ignored the demands of his biased boss. This new foreman, however, was severely intolerant of religion. When the young mason refused to throw away his religious articles, as ordered by Longange, the bigot attacked the youth. Longange tied up Isidore's hands and feet, stomped on his head, neck, and legs, and while two other workers held the defenseless man, Longange mercilessly beat him. The brute then dragged the youth to a rubber-processing room, and left him for dead.

When an inspector for the colonial company discovered Isidore's beaten body, the official rushed the badly bruised but still breathing young man to another plantation. The official did all that he could to restore the youth to good health. After surviving for six months, Isidore succumbed to his internal and external injuries.

21 ✢ Bl. Victoria Rasomanarivo

Place: *Antananarivo, Madagascar (now in the Malagasy Republic)*
Fame: *Loving wife and lay leader*

Having been born and raised in the local ancestral religion of her tribe, this Malagasy girl took Victoria (1848-1894) as her Christian name when she was baptized at age fifteen. To become Christian took great strength of will and faith because her family of influential political leaders opposed her and threatened her with ostracism from the family.

Christianity had been introduced as early as the sixteenth century into Madagascar, which in 1960 changed its name to the Malagasy Republic. Christianity, however, never sank deep roots there until late in the nineteenth century. Ancestral worship remained the dominant religion. As a matter of fact, when Victoria was born, Christianity had been outlawed for the previous fifteen years. One year after she was born, a general persecution against Christians was declared. The soldiers of Queen Ranavalona I (r. 1828-1861) rounded up over two thousand Christians and killed eighteen of them: four were burned alive and the remaining fourteen were thrown from a two-hundred-foot-high cliff. During Queen Ranavalona's long reign, approximately one million people died as a result of religious persecution, military campaigns, and intentional starving of perceived enemies. The queen's son succeeded her and, desiring to reverse his mother's bloody rule, he instituted immediately a policy of Westernization, which included religious toleration. Unfortunately, within two years, zenophobic enemies assassinated the Westernizing king.

Religious persecution, military battles, and political intrigue provided the context in which Victoria grew up. At thirteen, she expressed to her family the desire to be baptized. The family refused her permission. Her politically influential family could not accept that one of their own would convert to Christianity. On her mother's side of the family, Victoria's grandfather had been chief minister to the queen for over twenty years, and her uncle had served as prime minister for more than thirty years and had married three successive queens of Malagasy. On her father's side, her uncle was the current commander in chief of the army, and, since Victoria's father had died, head of her mother's household. Refused permission at thirteen, Victoria on her own requested and received baptism two years later in 1863. Within the next six months, she received also the sacraments of penance, Eucharist, and confirmation. Her independent decisions required deep faith and character.

> Victoria's family found that she remained steadfast against all their threats and their pleas that she turn from Catholicism. The ultimate threat was that she would have to forfeit the right to be buried in the family tomb. This, in Malagasy society, was the worst form of rejection possible, the gravest punishment that could be given to anyone. Victoria assured her relatives of her love for them but was adamant that she would remain a Catholic. . . . Deceased relatives are seen as having the power to influence the lives of their descendants and are duly involved and thanked. Regard for them and for ancestral traditions can be found in many aspects of Malagasy society, particularly medicine. Tied to this are elaborate rituals for burial. The means by which a person eventually joins

again his or her ancestors is seen as being through burial
in the family tomb.[2]

According to custom, husbands were chosen for Malagasy
girls. Victoria's family chose the prime minister's son Radriaka,
whom the official had fathered out of wedlock before he had
married any of his four successive wives, including his present
wife, the reigning queen. Radriaka turned out to be a dissolute
and drunken husband. Not only were his marital infidelities
publicly known, but also he occasionally brought home his
mistresses and women of one-night stands. For twenty-three
years, Victoria bore patiently and compassionately these repeated
insults. She genuinely loved her husband, even to the point of
performing the slave's task of washing his feet when he came
home, many times very late and very drunk. She successfully
urged him to receive baptism on his deathbed.

Her life, ever since her youth, exemplified Christian living.
Her daily religious practices included attending Mass and receiving Communion, praying the Rosary and reciting the Angelus,
and meditating many hours each day. She ate and drank sparingly,
even less so during Lent. The slaves who accompanied her since
her childhood and until her death praised her for assisting them
when they were too busy or too ill to complete their assigned
tasks. She regularly instructed these same slaves and other poor
persons in the Catholic faith. Although blessed with great wealth,
she herself dressed simply and refused to wear Western clothing,
which was the custom among her class. She gave generously to the
poor, the sick, and the imprisoned whatever they needed: money,
medicines, food, and clothing. She did not stand aloof because of
her position. "She made herself the servant of others and it was for
this above all that one had so much veneration for her."[3] Continu-
ously peaceful and happy, she beamed, so said her contemporaries,
with a face that observers described as radiant.

Late in life, she experienced the absence of priests from the island. At the beginning of 1883, the Malagasy government expelled the French Jesuits. Before departing the mission, the priests assigned overall care of the Church's presence and practices to Victoria. Laymen reported to her and received from her the guidance necessary for their continuing the evangelization on the island. On the first Sunday when the Jesuits were no longer present, the authorities locked the Catholic churches. "Victoria stood up defiantly in front of the doors, and defiantly told the authorities: 'You can put me to death, but you have no right to shut the church.' The doors were opened and Victoria led the people inside."[4] The anti-Christian persecution lasted for almost three years. During this period, Victoria made sure that Sunday prayer services and catechetical instructions were conducted in all the churches and that victims of persecution were defended. When a change in political and religious policy permitted, the Jesuits returned in 1886 and found the local Church thriving.

When Victoria died after a four-day illness, those who paid their respects to her represented the cross-section of the whole society whom she had served: Protestants and Catholics, rich and poor, the politically powerful queen and prime minister, and the politically powerless lepers. Contrary to her wishes and her family's original threats, she was buried in the family tomb.

24 ✛ Martyrs of Utica

Place: Utica (now in Tunisia)
Fame: Countless martyrs

The Roman Martyrology, St. Augustine, and the poet Prudentius wax eloquently and at length about the faithful Christians, who at Utica, which lies about twenty-five miles west of Carthage, suffered for the faith during the reign of the father-and-son co-emperors Valerian (253-260) and Gallienus (253-268). While the Roman Martyrology counts their number at three hundred, Augustine claims they numbered one hundred fifty-three persons. Prudentius writes that the martyrs, when hurled into a white-hot limekiln pit, had their ashes transformed by the heat into a solid white mass, thereby creating the name *Massa Candida*, which means "White Mass." "Prudentius refers to them thus: 'Whiteness [*candor*] possesses their bodies; purity [*candor*] bears their souls to heaven. Hence they have merited to be for ever called the White Mass [*Massa candida*].' "[5]

Historical research has clarified some details of the fact of a mass martyrdom at this location. No historical evidence, however, supports the claim that a mass murder occurred during the reign of Valerian. As to the number of martyrs, scholars have found no evidence to support the claim of three hundred martyrs and reject outright the claim of one hundred fifty-three, which appears to be simply an allusion to the number of fishes caught by the apostles at Jesus' instruction.[6] Scholars suggest today that the name *Massa Candida* describes the name of the site in which this event took place, rather than the event of the martyrs' death having given the place its name.

27 ✠ St. Monica

Place: Tagaste, Numidia (now in Algeria)
Fame: Wise wife and mother

Monica (c. 331–387) possessed strong faith, indefatigable hope, and resilient love; and she needed each. Her pagan husband was abusive and unfaithful. His cantankerous mother lived with the young couple. Monica's oldest child, the future St. Augustine, gave up his Christian faith, joined a heretical sect, moved in with a mistress, and fathered a child out of wedlock. Monica, however, by her tireless prayers, occasional tears, and continuous proddings, guided all three of these difficult persons to baptism in the Catholic Church.

Born and raised by Catholic parents at Tagaste, which is located approximately sixty miles west of Carthage, Monica grew up listening to the stories of her maternal grandmother, who had endured an earlier anti-Christian persecution. Monica's faith was formed at home. When she was of marrying age, Monica's parents chose a husband for her, as was the custom. They selected Patricius, a pagan official who was financially secure and well respected in the community. Shortly after their marriage, Patricius began to verbally abuse Monica. He also philandered regularly with other women. "She knew, she saw, but she kept quiet and suffered in silence. She prayed, and probably wept, but she realized that the religion of the pagans condoned great moral degradation."[7] Monica's situation was not dissimilar from that of other married women in the town. They soon sought out her advice on how to deal with their husbands, since despite so many trials Monica seemed to enjoy an inner peace. Monica advised these women not to argue with their husbands when the atmosphere was heated, but to wait until the next day when emotions had cooled. Eventually, in 370, one year before he died, Patricius and his mother, having been inspired by the example of Monica, converted to the Catholic faith.

Patricius and Monica had at least three children: Augustine; a daughter named Perpetua; and another son, Navigius. Navigius fathered three children: one son and two daughters. All three children dedicated their lives to God by serving in their uncle Augustine's church as subdeacons and a committed virgin. Perpetua married but was widowed shortly after her wedding. She then became a leader in a local women's monastery. Augustine was educated at Tagaste, then at neighboring Madaura, and eventually at metropolitan Carthage, where he excelled in the study of classical rhetoric: literature and language.

Monica grew increasingly concerned about her oldest son. At seventeen, when Augustine went to Carthage, he left behind not only his home but also his home-training in Catholic faith and morals. This brilliant student became enamored with the study of other sects and philosophies. He fancied himself an adherent of Manichaeanism, which religion he maintained for the next nine years. He took a mistress and fathered with her a son, Adeodatus, during the second year of their cohabitation. The couple remained together for fifteen years. When Augustine occasionally returned to Tagaste, he wearied his mother with seemingly interminable discussions about his religion to which he tried to convert her. So vexing had the situation become that Monica refused him permission at first to take meals at her table and eventually even to enter the home. This estrangement continued until she experienced a vision in which an angel assured her: "Your son shall be with you." When she told her son about this vision, he smugly interpreted it to mean not that he would convert to the Catholic religion but rather that she would convert to his religion. Monica shot back, "He did not say that I was with you, but that you were with me."[8]

After Augustine completed formal studies, he opened at Carthage a private school that students paid to attend. Disappointed by the students' lack of intellectual interest and disruptive behavior, the young teacher decided to leave Carthage for Rome, with the hope of finding more serious students there. In 383, at the age of twenty-nine, he left for the Eternal City. Although Monica had wanted to go with him, Augustine would not let her. The two argued. One day, under the guise of saying good-bye to a friend at the harbor, Augustine set sail for Rome. Undaunted, Monica came to Rome on her own. At Rome, Augustine found students who were able but unwilling to pay;

deceitfully they avoided paying what they owed him. In hopes of improving his situation, Augustine accepted the position of chair of rhetoric at the university at Milan. Again, Monica traveled behind her son.

At Milan, Augustine listened regularly to the rhetorically superlative homilies of the city's bishop, St. Ambrose. Not only did Augustine expose himself at church to good rhetoric but also to good instruction in the faith. A few years later, he announced that he wished to be baptized. Augustine, his friends, and Monica retired to a suburban retreat at Cassiciacum, near Milan. During the Easter Vigil in 387, Augustine received baptism in the Catholic Church.

Shortly after that Easter celebration, Monica desired to return home. She explained that she hoped to be buried eventually beside her husband. She and her two sons traveled from Cassiciacum to Ostia, which was the seaport for Rome. At Ostia, she became ill. A week later, she died there. Her parting request to Augustine was: "Remember me at the table of the Lord."[9]

27 ✣ St. Poemen

Place: *Deserts of Skete and Terenuthis, Egypt*
Fame: *Author of wise sayings*

Poemen (d. fifth century) and many of his brothers together left the world and went into the desert. The oldest brother, Anubis, and second oldest, Poemen, took turns in leading the monastic community of their brothers. Anubis wrote the rule with the assistance of his brothers. When Anubis died, Poemen took over sole authority for the community.

Poemen's sayings reveal a wisdom born of time and experience, of having faced one's own shortcomings, and of having shown compassion to others in the face of their shortcomings.

The monk manifests a profound insight into each person's relationship with God and with one another.

In *The Sayings of the Desert Fathers*, Poemen's sayings account for more than one fifth of the number of entries, and one seventh of the volume of the sayings. Some of Poemen's sayings are presented below.

> A man may seem to be silent, but if his heart is condemning others, he is babbling ceaselessly. But there may be another who talks from morning till night and yet he is truly silent; that is, he says nothing that is not profitable.[10]

> If a man has sinned and denies it, saying: "I have not sinned," do not reprimand him; for that will discourage him. But say to him, "Do not lose heart, brother, but be on guard in the future," and you will stir his soul to repentance.[11]

> If a man accuses himself, he is protected on all sides.[12]

> A brother questioned Abba Poemen saying, "If I see my brother committing a sin, is it right to conceal it?" The old man said to him, "At the very moment we hide our brother's fault, God hides our own and at the moment when we reveal our brother's fault, God reveals ours too."[13]

28 ✟ St. Augustine

Place: Hippo (now in Tunisia)
Fame: Father and Doctor of the Church

"Called Doctor of Grace, he [Augustine] is one of the greatest of the Fathers and Doctors of the Church, and with the possible exception of Thomas Aquinas, the greatest single intellect the Catholic Church has ever produced."[14]

Augustine (354-430) was born in the small town of Tagaste in the Roman province of Numidia. His parents were his Catholic mother, St. Monica, and his pagan father, Patricius, who converted just before his death in 371. Raised in the faith, Augustine was not baptized until adulthood, as was the custom. In his adolescent years, while studying sixty miles from home at the university at Carthage, he drifted from the belief in and practice of Catholicism.

Always a serious student in search of the truth, Augustine investigated various philosophical and quasi-religious systems, especially Manichaeanism, but also Aristotelianism, Stoicism, Pythagoreanism, Skepticism, and astrology. This open-ended search resulted in a real but vague belief in God. After a dozen years of teaching at Carthage, where his students were disinterested in learning, he moved to Rome, where his students were dishonest about paying for their classes. One year later, Augustine responded to a job opening for a teaching position at Milan and moved there in 384.

His conversion to Christianity occurred at Milan. There he encountered the repeated exhortations of his mother, Monica, and the preaching of the city's archbishop, St. Ambrose. Monica kept urging Augustine to send home to Africa his mistress of fifteen years and to marry someone of higher social status comparable to his own. Reluctantly the son yielded to the mother's plea, but then he found life so lonely that he took another mistress for two more years.

Ambrose taught a spiritual rather than a corporeal interpretation to explain the existence of God and the image of God in creation. This interpretation attracted Augustine. A lightbulb went on in his head, inspiring him to write, "I blushed joyfully."[15] He repented of the criticisms he had leveled against the Church's teachings because he had ridiculed them without having researched them. Even though Ambrose's use of Alexandrian spiritual exegesis and Neoplatonist language had enlightened Augustine, he still was not sufficiently inspired to become a Catholic. He hesitated to commit himself at this time because he had committed himself previously to so many other philosophies and quasi-religions. He believed in his head, but not yet in his heart. He continued to read Neoplatonist writings and the Scriptures.

One day, however, while sitting in a garden with his friend St. Alipius and reading St. Paul's letter to the Romans, Augustine was struck in his conscience by the immorality of his behaviors. "There arose a mighty storm, bringing with it a mighty downpour of tears,"[16] he writes. He stood up from his seat beside Alipius, walked to a private place, and threw himself down on the ground, crying inconsolably. The saint continues, "And lo, I heard from a nearby house, a voice like that of a boy or a girl, I know not which, chanting and repeating over and over, 'Take up and read. Take up and read.' "[17] With that instruction, he walked back to Alipius, picked up the text of St. Paul, and opened spontaneously to the words: "Let us live honorably as in the day, not in reveling and drunkenness, not in debauchery and licentiousness, not in quarreling and jealousy. Instead, put on the Lord Jesus Christ, and make no provision for the flesh, to gratify its desires."[18]

From that day forward in August of 386, Augustine changed his life. He gave up the study of law in favor of pursuing the monastic life. He canceled his wedding and marriage plans. He moved from Milan to its outskirts at Cassiciacum, where he gathered a community of disciples dedicated to prayer, penance, and study. At the beginning of Lent, he returned to Milan and enrolled himself, his son, Adeodatus, and his friend Alipius in the catechumenate program. At the Easter Vigil in 387, all three were baptized. A year later, he returned to Tagaste, where he and his followers settled down on a portion of his share of the family's estate. The newly baptized convert sold the remainder of his property and distributed the proceeds to the poor.

Priesthood was thrust upon Augustine by acclamation of the cathedral congregation at Hippo. Once, when Bishop Valerius was preaching about the community's responsibility to identify and supply priests for ordination, the congregation responded by seizing Augustine and submitting him for ordination. Valerius and Augustine agreed to this action, but Valerius permitted Augustine to continue his monasticism by providing him with a house and garden near the church. Contrary to custom, the bishop allowed Augustine to preach even though the bishop was present at the same services. This preaching experience made clear to Augustine how much he still needed to learn about the Scriptures. He requested and received permission to continue his education, along with his writing and preaching. Six years later, in 395, he was ordained coadjutor bishop.

For thirty-five years, Augustine served as bishop of Hippo, the most important see after Carthage in the Roman Empire's province of Africa. He established residence at the site of the cathedral and there created a community environment for his priests. He received visitors of every station in life, especially other bishops who sought his advice. He attended Church councils in Africa and other provinces. Augustine's writings that remain extant include almost a hundred treatises, over two hundred letters, over two hundred fifty sermons, and his most famous books, *Confessions* and *The City of God*. He met head-on the controversies of his day. Between 383 and 399, he challenged the Manichaeans; between 394 and 420, he published tracts against the Donatists; during the period 412 to 419, he confronted the Pelagians and Semi-Pelagians, and from 418 until his death, he refuted the Arians and Semi-Arians. In all his dealings, he is remembered for being particularly personal. "He marks all that he treats with that personal quality that is the product of a nature that is exceptionally sensitive, of an experience that is exceptionally lucid, and above all, of a love that is exceptionally profound. This personal consciousness is perhaps the most striking trait of his genius and the most decisive source of his influence upon our history."[19]

The last years of his long life were busy. In 426, he completed writing *The City of God* and began writing his *Retractions*, which is a critical review and revision of his previous writings. Recognizing his old age and the Church's need for a younger bishop, he named a successor. He chose the young deacon Heraclius and had the congregation acclaim the choice, but Augustine did not ordain him bishop; Augustine continued to serve as bishop until he died four years later. In that last year of Augustine's life, the Vandals swept across the north coast of Africa from Tingis to Hippo. These barbarian invaders, who had been invited into Africa to protect Count Boniface's interests against Roman threats, turned against their host. During the third month of their siege, with the barbarians literally knocking at the city gates, Augustine died.

28 ✛ St. Moses the Black

Place: Desert of Skete, Egypt
Fame: Convert from thievery to Christianity

One of the most famous Desert Fathers at the monastery of Petra at Skete was Moses the Egyptian (c. 330–c. 405), who converted from a life of crime to a life of holiness. Prior to his conversion, he worked as a servant in the home of a wealthy Egyptian. Because of repeated thefts from his employer, Moses was dismissed from his job. On the streets, he gathered a gang of like-minded thieves, who thrived on crimes against people and property. Moses' ferocity is legendary. One story follows.

> Once some contemplated villainy was spoiled by the barking of a sheep-dog giving the alarm, and Moses swore to kill the shepherd. To get at him he had to swim across the Nile with his sword in his teeth, but the shepherd had hidden himself by burrowing into the sand; Moses could not find him, so he made up for it by killing four rams, tying them together and towing them back across the river. Then he flayed the rams, cooked and ate the best parts, sold the skins for wine, and walked fifty miles to join his fellows. That was the sort of man Moses was.[20]

No details are known about Moses' conversion. Hagiographers suggest that, while hiding out in the desert at Nitria, he witnessed the example of the monks. He abandoned his villainous ways for the virtues of the monastery. He was ordained by Theophilus, the archbishop of Alexandria, whence he retreated to the desert at Skete. He became renowned for his love of solitude and expressions of mercy. He also suffered on account of the color of his skin. Two stories from *The Sayings of the Desert Fathers* exemplify his compassion and his experience of racism.

> A brother at Scetis [Skete] committed a fault. A council was called to which Abba Moses was invited, but he refused to go to it. Then the priest sent someone to say to him, "Come, for everyone is waiting for you." So, he got up and went. He took a leaking jug, filled it with water and carried it with him. The others came out to meet him and said to him, "What is this, Father?" The old man said to them, "My sins run out behind me, and I do not see them, and today I am coming to judge the errors of

another." When they heard that, they said no more to the brother but forgave him.[21]

Another day when a council was being held in Scetis, the Fathers treated Moses with contempt, in order to test him, saying, "Why does this black man come among us?" When he heard this, he kept silence. When the council was dismissed, they said to him, "Abba, did that not grieve you at all?" He said to them, "I was grieved, but I kept silence."[22]

Another day, while he and other monks were peacefully going about their routine of prayer and work, Berber marauders attacked. It is said that "Moses refused to allow his monks to defend themselves but made them run away before it was too late: All that take the sword shall perish with the sword. He remained, and seven with him, and all save one were murdered by the infidels."[23]

30 ✟ Bl. Ghebre Michael

Place: Godjam, Ethiopia
Fame: Monophysite monk who became a Catholic priest and martyr

When the Vatican Office of the Propagation of the Faith re-opened its mission to Ethiopia in 1838, after sporadic evangelization since the thirteenth century and official closure in 1717, no one imagined that two saintly persons would emerge almost immediately from that mission initiative. Justin de Jacobis, an Italian missionary priest, and his protégé Ghebre Michael (c. 1790-1855), a learned Ethiopian monk who converted from Monophysitism to Catholicism, were respectively canonized in 1975 and beatified in 1926.

For about a dozen years prior to 1839, the Coptic episcopal see in Ethiopia had remained vacant. King Oubie and other Ethiopian leaders desired that someone be appointed, and perhaps even an Ethiopian rather than an Egyptian as always had been the case. For this delicate mission the king selected distinguished delegates, including Ghebre and Justin. The king invited the recently arrived Justin to lead the mission because it was thought that an educated European would increase the likelihood not only of a safe journey through the slave-trading Muslim territory but also of favorable reception by the Orthodox patriarch of Alexandria, who resided at Cairo. The Italian Vincentian priest agreed to join the delegation as long as the king agreed to recommend to the patriarch that the priest might establish Catholic churches in Ethiopia and that the entourage would continue their journey to visit the pope at Rome. In January 1841, the group left Ethiopia and arrived three months later at Cairo. There the patriarch not only unilaterally imposed on them a young Egyptian bishop named Salama but also threatened with excommunication those who would dare to visit the pope. The delegates were so discouraged at the failed results of the mission that, believing they had nothing else to lose, they continued on to the Holy City.

Along the journey Ghebre Michael grew to perceive the Catholic faith and its representatives in a new light. Ghebre and Justin delighted in conversation about faith and religion and the theological similarities and dissimilarities between Monophysitism and Catholicism. Ghebre had been impressed, too, by the pope, who warmly welcomed the entourage and celebrated the liturgy with them. On the journey home through the Holy Land, the Catholic missionary and the Monophysite monk continued their conversations. A friendship took root. So, too, did Ghebre's interest in the Catholic Church.

The delegation had been absent from Ethiopia for one-and-a-half years. Meanwhile, the political climate had changed drastically. King Oubie was being challenged politically by Salama, a popular bishop. Salama, fearing Ghebre's opposition to his appointment as metropolitan, ordered that Ghebre be captured and killed. Ghebre, on the advice of Justin, avoided capture by hopscotching home surreptitiously from monastery to monastery. Ghebre even surprised Salama by appearing at an assembly called by the metropolitan. Delivering the Arabic-written patriarchal document from Cairo to Salama, Ghebre waited expectantly for Salama to read aloud the document. Instead, Salama read it privately and pocketed it. When Ghebre and others threatened to refuse to recognize Salama as metropolitan, a riot erupted. Ghebre suffered his first of many beatings.

Rejected by the arrogant leaders of the Orthodox religion and impressed by the truthfulness and kindness of Justin and the pope, Ghebre in September 1843 requested to be baptized by Justin. After the two had devoted further time to studies and discussions in preparation for the sacrament, Justin baptized Ghebre in February 1844.

Ghebre dedicated himself to the Catholic mission in Ethiopia. He established a seminary for native vocations and translated the Roman catechism and various theological treatises into the three Ethiopian languages of Amharic, Gheez, and Tigre. Ghebre's special calling was to discuss theological and spiritual issues with the local clergy and to win converts among them to the truth of Catholicism. By the end of one year, fifteen Monophysite priests had converted. Oftentimes, when the priests converted, so did their entire congregations. Since the priests' ordinations were not recognized as valid, a Catholic bishop ordained the converted priests when he visited Ethiopia in October 1846. Salama grew increasingly restless at the success of the Catholic mission, which impeded his goals of fostering political unity by requiring religious unity.

Salama initiated a persecution against the Catholics. He

threatened with death anyone who dared to assist the Catholics with even so much as a glass of water. In October 1848, the bishop expelled Justin from Ethiopia. The burgeoning group of Catholics, including Ghebre, fled to the remote and rugged mountains of Choos. Many neophyte Catholics apostatized under threats from Salama. Ghebre, however, continued his hidden ministry of evangelization and formation. At the capital city of Gondar, Ghebre was instructing the clergy when he was captured by Salama's soldiers and was imprisoned for seventy days. King Oubie, a former student of the former Orthodox monk, intervened to gain Ghebre's release. Three years later, in 1851, on the first day of the New Year, Justin, who secretly had been ordained a bishop, surreptitiously ordained his first native vocation, Ghebre Michael. Again Ghebre returned to Gondar, this time to convert not the clergy, but King Oubie. Ghebre believed that many educated persons would follow the Catholic faith if the king himself converted. Salama's political power was too great, however, and Oubie, fearing political revolution from Salama, deferred requesting baptism.

Revolution erupted in 1850, when a third political leader named Cassa joined the struggle for power. Cassa sided with Salama against Oubie. Cassa offered to kill Ghebre and other Catholics and to destroy all Catholic religious and educational institutions in exchange for Salama's declaring Cassa as "King of the Kings of Ethiopia." Salama agreed. In July 1854, Justin and Ghebre and four other Catholics were arrested at Gondar. Having been placed in separate prisons, the master and his disciple never saw each other again. After four months, Justin was exiled to the frontier town of Senaar, but in the process of transfer, the Muslim guards who received him released him. Months later, he arrived at the safe-haven coastal town of Massawa.

Meanwhile, soldiers under orders from Bishop Salama repeatedly interrogated and cruelly tortured Ghebre for the next eleven months. He was placed in isolation in a completely darkened dungeon, where he was denied food and drink for days on end. After the first few months, Salama sent the old man to Cassa, who agreed to kill the sexagenarian. Cassa's soldiers whipped and beat Ghebre. He refused, however, to relinquish his faith or to die. Exasperated, in March 1855, Cassa ordered Ghebre to be beaten again.

> Four tormentors received orders to strike him with the tail of a giraffe whose long hairs resembled wire. These scourgers, relaying each other, two by two, struck the sufferer with his face against the ground. To the strokes continuing to fall upon his bruised flesh, he replied in a strong voice: "I believe in the faith of the Holy Church, Catholic, Apostolic and Roman! O my God, I beg you to assist me by your grace and receive me in your great mercy!"
>
> The tyrant, seeing himself vanquished, ordered that the prisoner should receive seventy strokes on his eyes. Under the shock of the rods, the blood gushed from the orbits. "Are you tired?" "Strike! But do strike," shouted the tyrant, "strike until he is dead!" According to the testimony of witnesses, other torturers replaced the first who were exhausted; they rained blows upon the body of the martyr with such fury that it was impossible to count their number. Although they replaced each other, they had to give up as harvesters who drop the flail when the wheat is threshed. The sufferer lay there; they believed him dead. He was waiting![24]

Ghebre picked himself up off the ground and walked to his cell. Later, Ghebre was brought to trial. Because he remained steadfast in his faith, he was ordered to be shot to death. He was dragged to the place of execution. The crowds, however, wept for his life and an English official begged for the old man's release. Weeks later, however, broken in health, chained in leg-irons, propped up against a tree, and still firm in his Catholic faith, Ghebre breathed his last.

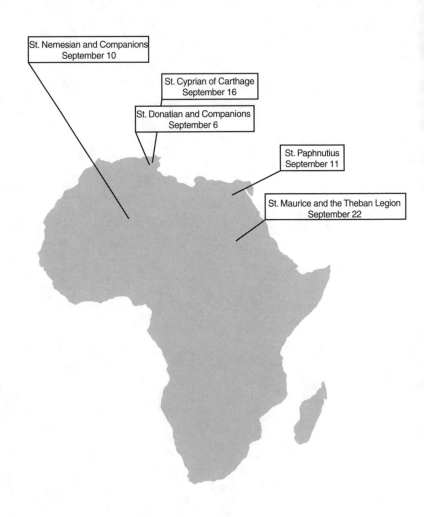

St. Nemesian and Companions
September 10

St. Cyprian of Carthage
September 16

St. Donatian and Companions
September 6

St. Paphnutius
September 11

St. Maurice and the Theban Legion
September 22

SEPTEMBER

6 ✝ St. Donatian and Companions

Place: *Vandal kingdom of Africa (now in Algeria, Tunisia, and Libya)*
Fame: *Martyred by barbarian Vandals*

In 429, the governor of the Roman province of Africa, Count Boniface, invited the barbarian Vandals to leave the province of Gaul (now France) and come to northern Africa to assist him in his civil war against the Roman empress Galla Placidia. In the short term this strategy proved highly successful, as the horde of eighty thousand Vandals crushed the military forces of the empress. In the long term, however, the strategy backfired when the Vandals refused to leave. They conquered not only the empress's army but also at the end of ten years the Roman revolutionaries who had invited them. The Vandals gained control, therefore, of the thousand-mile coast of northern Africa, stretching from the province of Mauretania Caesaria on the Atlantic Ocean over to the western border of the province of Cyrenaica. Some historians claim that the Vandals' sweeping success was aided by the native Berbers' dissatisfaction with foreign Romans, the Roman landowners' dissatisfaction with imperial taxes, and the ongoing rebellion fomented by the oppressed Donatists.

The successive father-and-son Vandal leaders, namely Genseric (r. 428-477) and Huneric (r. 477-484), imposed their heretical Arian faith on the peoples whom they conquered. In 484, Huneric ordered that all Catholic Christian churches were to be closed and that the property of the clergy was to be given over to the Arian Christian clergy. The Catholic bishops protested this command and appealed to the ruler. Huneric met these bishops outside the walls of the city, but his response to their plea was to order his soldiers to "ride them down."[1] With that, Donatian (d. 484) and four other bishops accompanying him were chased by horsemen from the environs of the city to the desert, where the bishops succumbed to hunger, thirst, and exposure.

Fifty miles southeast of Carthage, at the coastal city of Leptis Minor, Huneric ordered that the local bishop, Laetus (d. 484), be thrown into a dungeon as punishment for his opposition to Arian teachings. After some days, the bishop was retrieved from jail and burned alive.

10 ✠ St. Nemesian and Companions

Place: Numidia (now in Algeria)
*Fame: Corresponded with Cyprian about their
impending martyrdoms*

In the Roman province of Numidia, Bishop Nemesian and eight other bishops, plus countless priests, deacons, and laypersons, suffered martyrdom under the eighth general imperial persecution that Valerian led beginning in 257. The governor of Numidia had rounded up local Christians and tortured them. Some of these faithful died. Others were sent to mines and marble quarries as far away as Sigum, at Nicomedia (now Turkey) on the Black Sea. "Out of this holy company some were taken at intervals to be tormented afresh or inhumanely butchered, whilst others continued their lingering martyrdom in hunger, nakedness, and filth, exhausted with hard labour, persecuted with daily blows, hardships, and insults."[2] Most died from the wounds and injuries, which they received from their harsh mistreatment.

Cyprian, the metropolitan bishop, who had already been exiled from Carthage fifty miles southwest to Curubis, wrote to these persecuted Christians. They replied through their bishop, Nemesian, that they had been inspired and encouraged by Cyprian's example and letter. Cyprian's public profession of faith even in the hostile environment of the imperial court inspired subsequent Christian prisoners similarly to profess their faith. The letter from Nemesian and his companions concludes, "Let us assist one another by our prayers, that God and Christ and the whole choir of angels may send us help when we shall most want it."[3]

11 ✢ St. Paphnutius

Place: Upper Thebaid, Egypt
Fame: Opponent of imposing on clerics the law of celibacy

As a young man, Paphnutius (d.c. 350) passed many years in the desert as a disciple of St. Antony. Later he was ordained a bishop in the Upper Thebaid. During the persecution of Emperor Maximinus Daia (r. 310-313), the bishop suffered the common torture of having his left leg mutilated and his right eye torn out, after which he was exiled to work in the neighboring mines. When Christians were permitted to practice their religion once again, the bishop returned to his see. Welcomed back on account of his heroic sufferings and sanctity, he took up again the defense of the Church against the Arian heresy. He attended the Church's first ecumenical council, held at Nicaea in 325. Ten years later, he attended the Council of Tyre, where he persuaded Maximus, the bishop of Jerusalem, to come to his senses and separate himself from his Arian companions.

Paphnutius, a man who had observed the strictest continence all his life, is said to have distinguished himself at the council (Nicaea) by his opposition to clerical celibacy. Many of the bishops were for making a general law forbidding all bishops, priests, deacons and subdeacons to live with wives whom they had married before their ordination. Whereupon Paphnutius rose up in the assembly and opposed the motion, saying that it was enough to conform to the ancient tradition of the Church, which forbade the clergy marrying after their ordination. For the married use of wedlock is chastity, he reminded the fathers, and implored them not to lay the yoke of separation on clerics and their wives. St. Paphnutius carried the council with him, and to this day it is the law of the Eastern Churches, whether Catholic or dissident, that married men may receive all holy orders below the episcopate, and continue to live freely with their wives.[4]

16 ☩ St. Cyprian of Carthage

Place: *Carthage (now in Tunisia)*
Fame: *Father and Doctor of the Church, bishop and martyr*

Within the dozen years between his conversion from paganism to Christianity, that is, 246 to 258, Cyprian (c. 200-258) earned the honorary titles of Father and Doctor of the Church for his pastoral leadership and theological teachings.

Having been well educated, Cyprian became a rhetorician, teacher, and lawyer before being ordained a priest and later elected as bishop. He attributed his conversion to the example and insights of an old priest named Caecilius.

Controversy swirled throughout Cyprian's ten-year tenure

as bishop. No sooner had he been ordained bishop in 248, than Emperor Decius (r. 249-251) decreed an anti-Christian persecution in 249. Cyprian fled for his life. Only when the persecution ended in 251 did the bishop return. What he discovered was a Church in turmoil. A schismatic bishop named Novatian was permitting the *lapsi*, that is, those Christians who had succumbed to the pressures to offer sacrifices to the Roman gods, to return to the Church without having performed some suitable penance for their defection. Cyprian, asserting his authority, convened three regional councils within the next two years to determine appropriate penances for the *lapsi*, an appropriate penalty for Novatian, and a declaration in favor of papal supremacy over other ecclesiastical sees. Cyprian delivered his famous lecture, *De Unitate Ecclesiae,* at this time. Novatian fled to Rome, where he joined the antipope Novatius in attempts to weaken the see of Rome.

Back in Carthage, Cyprian had his hands full assisting victims of a plague that besieged the city from 252 to 254. Despite the Church's practical assistance, Christians in general and Cyprian in particular were blamed for the severity of the plague. During this crisis, the bishop wrote *De mortalite* for the benefit of his flock.

Although Cyprian had defended both papal supremacy and Pope Cornelius during the *lapsi* question, Cyprian ran afoul of both the papacy and Pope Stephen during the rebaptism controversy. The new pope had declared valid the baptisms administered by heretics and schismatics, since the power lay within Christ and not the particular priest as agent. Cyprian thought and taught otherwise. He asked: How could someone who had demonstrated opposition to the Church be the agent for welcoming people into that Church? Cyprian argued vociferously and within the space of two years, 255 and 256, he convened his bishops in the Roman province of Africa to three councils, all of which reaffirmed Cyprian's position. The bishop failed to see the contradiction between his stance in support of papal supremacy in 251 and his opposition to the supremacy of papal teaching in 256. The bitter dispute reached its denouement when Pope Stephen threatened the great Bishop Cyprian with excommunication if he continued to hold his position.

The papal threat became a moot point when Emperor Valerian (253-260), in 257, unleashed a two-pronged anti-Christian persecution. In the first year and first stage, all bishops, priests, and deacons were mandated to participate in Roman religious services. When Cyprian refused, he was arrested and exiled to the town of Curubis. In the second stage and second year, all bishops, priests, and deacons were ordered to be executed. When Cyprian was brought before the Roman proconsul, he held to his faith in Jesus and the Church that Jesus had founded. On September 14, 258, Cyprian was beheaded.

> The proconsul consulted his assessor. He then pronounced sentence, very reluctantly, as follows: "You have long lived an irreligious life; you have gathered round you many members of a wicked association; you have set yourself up against the Roman gods and their religion; and you have rejected the call of our pious and most sacred emperors, the *Augusti* Valerian and Gallienus and the most noble *Caesar* Valerian, to the observance of their rites. Accordingly, since you are found guilty of being the author and leader of most shameful crimes, you shall be made an example to those whom you have associated with yourself in wickedness; the law must be vindicated in your blood. (Here he read from his tablets.) "We order that Thascius Cyprianus be put to death by the sword." And Cyprian answered, "Thanks be to God."

When they heard this sentence, the assembled brethren cried out, "Let us too be beheaded with him!" and amid a tumult the crowd went along with him to the place of execution. Cyprian was taken to the field of Sextus, where people had climbed into trees to get a better view. He took off his cloak and knelt down, bowing in prayer to the Lord. Then he took off his tunic, handing it to his deacons, and stood up in his linen undergarment to wait for the executioner; on his arrival Cyprian directed that twenty-five gold coins be given him. The brethren spread linen cloths on the ground around their bishop, and he blindfolded himself, but he could not tie the ends of the handkerchief and a priest and a subdeacon, both named Julian, did it for him. Thus did blessed Cyprian suffer.[5]

22 ✣ St. Maurice and the Theban Legion

Place: *Thebes, Lower Egypt*
Fame: *Christian soldiers refused to sacrifice to Roman gods*

Far from their native Thebes in Lower Egypt, Maurice (d.c. 287) and his fellow soldiers died as martyrs near Lake Geneva at what is now known as St. Maurice-en-Valais (in present-day Switzerland). Maurice's legion, which numbered sixty-six hundred men, had been conscripted in Thebes. Under the rule of Emperor Maximian (r. 286–305), they marched from the province of Egypt to the distant Rhône River, where they encountered barbarian Gauls encroaching upon the river border that separated the imperial and barbarian territories.

In preparing to meet the enemy, the emperor ordered all his troops to offer sacrifice to the Roman gods to invoke success for their attack. As other legions prepared to worship, the

Theban legion withdrew from what is now Martigny to the current St. Maurice. When the emperor inquired about their conduct, he was informed of their refusal to sacrifice to the Roman gods. The emperor then confronted the entire legion. Asked why they refused to sacrifice, their commander and spokesman, Maurice, reportedly gave the following discourse.

> We are your soldiers, but also the soldiers of the true God. We owe you military service and obedience; but we cannot renounce Him who is our Creator and Master, and also yours even though you reject Him. In all things which are not against His law we must willingly obey you, as we have done hitherto. We readily oppose all your enemies, whoever they are; but we cannot dip our hands into the blood of innocent persons. We have taken an oath to God before we took one to you: you can place no confidence in our second oath if we violate the first. You command us to punish the Christians; behold, we are such. We confess God the Father, author of all things, and His Son, Jesus Christ. We have seen our companions slain without lamenting them, and we rejoice at their honour. Neither this nor any other provocation has tempted us to revolt. We have arms in our hands, but we do not resist because we would rather die innocent than live by any sin.[6]

Maximian threatened that he would decimate the legion if they failed to offer sacrifice. Unanimously, the legion refused. The remainder of the account is questioned by scholars because of the alleged magnitude and severity of the emperor. According to St. Eucherius, who wrote this story in approximately 434, after the first decimation occurred, the emperor ordered another and then another decimation until the entire legion was wiped out. Some scholars find it difficult to believe that the emperor would have killed so many of his own soldiers. Scholars argue that the extent of cruelty is hard to believe, that no other physical or literary evidence exists to support this story, and that the emperor would not have been likely to slaughter his own men whom he needed to wipe out the barbarians. While the exact number of martyrs is questioned, the fact that Maurice and members of his legion were martyred is not questioned.

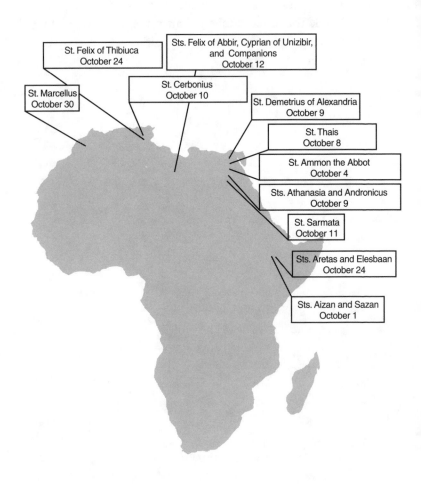

St. Felix of Thibiuca
October 24

Sts. Felix of Abbir, Cyprian of Unizibir,
and Companions
October 12

St. Cerbonius
October 10

St. Marcellus
October 30

St. Demetrius of Alexandria
October 9

St. Thais
October 8

St. Ammon the Abbot
October 4

Sts. Athanasia and Andronicus
October 9

St. Sarmata
October 11

Sts. Aretas and Elesbaan
October 24

Sts. Aizan and Sazan
October 1

OCTOBER

1 ✠ Sts. Aizan and Sazan

Place: *Abyssinia (now Ethiopia)*
Fame: *Brother martyrs*

These brothers died for the faith around the turn of the fifth century. They were friends of St. Athanasius and avid evangelizers of the faith.

4 ✠ St. Ammon the Abbot

Place: *Nitrian desert, Egypt*
Fame: *Married man turned monk*

After his wealthy parents died, his uncle and other relatives of Ammon (d.c. 350) pressured him into marrying. Married at twenty-two, but motivated by St. Paul's stated preference for the celibate life over married life, Ammon and his wife lived as brother and sister for the next eighteen years.[1] The couple practiced great self-discipline not only in sex but also in diet and dedication to prayer. After his relatives died, Ammon and his wife separated amicably so that each one might dedicate his and her remaining years to the monastic life. He left home and pursued the hermit's life in the Nitrian desert, a barren and poisonous marshland seventy miles southwest of Alexandria. She remained at home and invited a number of like-minded religious women to join her in the religious life. Ammon returned home to visit his wife about once every six months.

Because of his reputation for holiness, Ammon attracted

many disciples among the hermits already living in the desert. These men continued their solitary lives, while on occasion seeking out the guidance of Ammon. Even the revered St. Antony visited the newest Desert Father. Antony advised Ammon to form a community with his disciples, whereby they would forgo their solitary eremetical life in order to experience the communal cenobitical life. Antony suggested that while the monks had lived alone and occasionally visited Ammon, they might live together and occasionally return to their individual cells. The purpose, Antony proposed, was to provide mutual support within the difficult monastic lifestyle. Antony became the spiritual father of Ammon's community.

Radiant in prayer, austere in diet, allegedly a miracle worker, Ammon became renowned for holiness by those who knew him.

8 ✢ St. Thais

Place: Alexandria, Egypt
Fame: Prostitute turned hermitess

Historians question the truthfulness of this story because the facts are hard to come by, specific individuals are called by many different names, the public accepted it widely and uncritically, and the story never originated until two centuries after the alleged characters had died.

A prostitute named Thais (fourth century) made her living in the capital city of Alexandria. Her trade earned her a great deal of wealth. One day she met a monk who converted her to Christianity; in various renditions of the story the monk is identified as either St. Bessarion, St. Paphnutius, or St. Serapion. The woman left her trade, distributed her wealth to the poorest of the poor, and presented herself to a women's monastery. There she walled up herself in her solitary cell, thinking herself unworthy to interact with the nuns. She dedicated her life there to performing penance in reparation for her past sins.

On the advice of St. Antony the abbot, she ended her confinement after three years. She mingled among the nuns of the convent. After fifteen days, however, she died unexpectedly.

9 ✣ Sts. Athanasia and Andronicus

Place: Alexandria, Egypt
Fame: Married couple turned monks

This native Alexandrian couple (fifth century) moved to Antioch of Syria, where Andronicus plied his trade as silversmith. The husband and wife raised two children. Suddenly, when the couple had been married a dozen years, both children died on the same day. Once, while passing many hours praying at the children's graveside, Athanasia experienced a vision of their children in heaven. Confident in that consolation, she hurried to her husband. She suggested and he concurred that they abandon the secular world, return to their homeland, and dedicate to God the remainder of their lives.

In the desert of Skete, they encountered the venerable St. Daniel of Many Miracles. He directed Andronicus to reside at the monastery at Tabennisi, and Athanasia to live as a hermitess at Skete, but for safety's sake, to be dressed as a man.

9 ✣ St. Demetrius of Alexandria

Place: Alexandria, Egypt
Fame: Early defender and later critic of Origen

Allegedly St. Mark the Evangelist's eleventh successor as bishop of Alexandria, Demetrius (126-231) was the first bishop for whom external evidence supports the claim that he was bishop there. Appointed bishop in 189, he served for forty-three years until he died at the age of one hundred five.

Bishop Demetrius is famous for his dealings with his even more famous subject, Origen. When St. Clement resigned as head of the catechetical school at Alexandria, Demetrius is believed by many but not all scholars to have appointed Origen as the successor. All scholars agree, however, that when Origen castrated himself in response to the Gospel mandate "If your right eye causes you to sin, tear it out and throw it away; . . . and if your right hand causes you to sin, cut it off and throw it away,"[2] Demetrius defended the overzealous Origen. Later, however, Demetrius joined the ranks of critics of Origen. In 215, this layman overstepped his authority by preaching in the churches of Palestine, even though, admittedly, it was the bishops of Caesarea in Palestine who had invited him. In 230, these same bishops of Caesarea overstepped their bounds by ordaining Origen without having sought or having received the required permission of Origen's local bishop, Demetrius. Consequently, Demetrius convened a diocesan synod that condemned Origen, deposed him from the priesthood, and ordered him not to preach.

10 ✛ St. Cerbonius

Place: *Vandal kingdom of Africa (now Algeria, Tunisia, and Libya)*
Fame: *Persecuted by barbarian tribes*

Three barbarian tribes threatened Bishop Cerbonius (d.c. 575): the Vandals exiled him from northern Africa; the Ostrogoths condemned him to death at his new residence in Tuscany; the Lombards subsequently invaded Tuscany and exiled him to the island of Elba.

In his *Dialogues*, St. Gregory the Great relates the following story about Cerbonius at Tuscany.[3] It seems that during the Ostrogoths' invasion of Populonia, Cerbonius provided safe shelter to some Roman soldiers. As a penalty for the bishop's having aided the enemy, the Ostrogoth chief ordered that the cleric be killed by a bear in the public arena. In the arena, however, the bear did nothing more than lick the feet of the bishop. The disgusted chief then freed Cerbonius. The bishop chose to remain in the city.

Years later, when the Lombards replaced the Ostrogoths, who had moved farther west into what is now France, Cerbonius was captured and exiled to the island of Elba. There he remained for thirty years, teaching and preaching the faith. When the elderly bishop died, the townsfolk of Populonia traveled to Elba, retrieved the saint's body, and returned home to bury their beloved bishop.

11 ✟ St. Sarmata

Place: Thebaid, Egypt
Fame: Martyred

As one of the early disciples of St. Antony, Sarmata (also spelled Sarmatas), who died in 357, lived near his master in the desert on Mount Clisma near the Red Sea. He was renowned for his mortifications and great wisdom. A handful of sayings are attributed to him in *The Sayings of the Desert Fathers*. A few selections follow.

Abba Sarmatas said, "I prefer a sinful man who knows he has sinned and repents, to a man who has not sinned and considers himself to be righteous."[4]

They said of Abba Sarmatas that on Abba Poemen's

advice he was often alone for forty days. He completed this time as though he had done nothing special. Abba Poemen went to see him and said to him, "Tell me what you have seen by giving yourself such great hardship." The other said to him, "Nothing special." Abba Poemen said to him, "I shall not let you go till you tell me." Then he said, "I have discovered one simple thing: that if I say to my sleep, 'Go,' it goes, and if I say to it, 'Come,' it comes."[5]

Abba Sarmatas also said, "If a man does not flee from everything possible, he makes sin inevitable."[6]

Sarmata died when a group of Bedouins accosted and killed him in his desert dwelling.

12 ✢ Sts. Felix of Abbir, Cyprian of Unizibir, and Companions

Place: *Vandal kingdom of Africa (now in Libya)*
Fame: *Martyred by Huneric*

The Vandal king Huneric (r. 477–484) received from his father Genseric (r. 428–477) both his Arian religion and his hatred of Catholicism. The heretics despised the orthodox Christians. Victor of Vita reports that Huneric ordered many hundreds of Catholics to be force-marched into the desert of Libya. Soldiers corralled the Catholics into overcrowded and underequipped jails. When the jails were bursting with prisoners, the soldiers released them in the direction of the desert, running behind the Christians, and stabbing and pricking them with pointed spears. Other victims had their legs roped together, were tied to the backs of horses, and were dragged across rocky ground, with their flesh tearing and bones breaking in the process. Meanwhile, onlookers hurled stones at the innocents being exiled. With one group exiled, the soldiers rounded up additional Catholics to set in motion another wave of victims.

Throughout this persecution, the bishops Felix of Abbir (d.c. 484) and Cyprian of Unizibir (d.c. 484) attempted to comfort the members of their congregations. They prayed with those about to be exiled and with those about to be left behind. All told, the martyred bishops, priests, deacons, and laity numbered 4,966 persons, of whom the overwhelming majority were lay members of the Church.

Soldiers questioned whether or not the elderly Felix, who already had served forty-four years as bishop, should be exiled because the aged and infirm man was incapable of walking far and would die soon anyway. An eyewitness reports, "The tyrant is said to have spoken in a rage: 'If he cannot sit on an animal, let untamed bulls be yoked to take him where I have ordered by dragging him along, fastened with ropes.' We bound him crossways on a mule like the trunk of a tree, and in this manner we carried him with us for the whole journey."[7]

24 ✛ Sts. Aretas and Elesbaan

Place: Ethiopia
Fame: Victim and avenger respectively in
military battles against Jews

The sixth-century Ethiopians Aretas (d. 521) and Elesbaan (d. 532) represent, in the first case, leaders among the Christians abused by an enemy; and in the second case, revered avengers of those abuses who cruelly abused the former victors.

The Aksumite Ethiopians had expanded their presence and power across the Red Sea into the region of Himyar (now

Yemen). The leader of the displaced people, himself known as Dhu Nowas (oftentimes transliterated as Dunaan), eventually rose up in rebellion against the foreign rulers. Dunaan, who had converted earlier to Judaism, captured the city of Zafar and slaughtered all the clergy and military there. He proceeded onto Najran, where, after a fierce battle, the Christians, led by Aretas, accepted Dunaan's offer of amnesty. The amnesty was immediately reneged on, with Dunaan beheading all the soldiers and burning alive in a pit all the clergy and consecrated virgins. When Aretas's wife refused the sexual advances of Dunaan, he executed her daughters in front of the mother, poured their blood down her throat, and beheaded her. All told, four thousand men, women, and children were killed.

News of this atrocity quickly spread in all directions: Persia, Syria, Egypt, and back home at Ethiopia. The patriarch of Alexandria suggested a permanent commemoration at Mass for those massacred. The patriarch went further, and along with the emperor, wrote to Aksumite King Elesbaan that military justice ought to be brought to bear upon Dunaan and by extension to the elders of the Jewish school at Tiberias, whom the patriarch held indirectly responsible. Elesbaan marched into Najran and recovered the kingdom for the Aksumites. "He restored Najran and installed a bishop sent from Alexandria, but both in the field and in dealing with the Jews who had encouraged the massacre he conducted himself with that cruelty and rapacity which are only to be looked for in the barbarous prince of a semi-pagan nation."[8] Toward the end of his life, Elesbaan forsook his political power, donated his crown to the Church of the Holy Sepulchre at Jerusalem, and retired to the desert as a hermit.

Interestingly, these two sainted Ethiopian Christians were probably adherents of the Monophysite heresy.

24 ✣ St. Felix of Thibiuca

Place: Carthage (now in Tunisia)
Fame: Martyr

One of the first Christians to die during the Diocletian (r. 284–305) persecution in Africa was Felix (d. 303), the bishop of Thibiuca. The bishop held firm to his faith during succeeding interrogations before three successive Roman officials: the Roman magistrate at Thibiuca, the legate in charge of the prison at Carthage, and finally the proconsul at Carthage. The following dialogue took place during Felix's arrest.

"Hand over whatever books or parchments you possess," said the magistrate Magnilianus.

"I have them," answered Bishop Felix, "but I will not give them up."

The magistrate Magnilianus said: "Hand the books over to be burned."

"It would be better for me to be burned," answered Bishop Felix, "rather than the divine Scriptures. For it is better to obey God rather than men."

The magistrate Magnilianus said: "The emperor's orders come before anything you say."

Bishop Felix answered: "God's commands come before those of men."

Magnilianus said: "Take three days to reconsider this."[9]

Three days later, the magistrate summoned the bishop. The request and the refusal were both repeated. The magistrate then sent Felix under the watchful eye of a court attendant to Carthage. There the local legate received the prisoner and threw him in jail. The next day, the legate asked Felix, "Why do you not surrender these useless writings?"[10] Again Felix refused to allow the Scriptures to be burned. The legate summarily dismissed the bishop to the lowest part of the prison. Sixteen days later, the proconsul Anulinus interrogated Felix. Again, the bishop refused to release the texts. The proconsul then ordered Felix to be beheaded immediately.

Another rendition of the story reports that Felix was martyred not in Africa but in Italy. After having refused to hand over the texts, Felix was placed in irons and imprisoned in a dungeon for nine days. He was then sent north to stand trial before the prefect Maximianus (r. 286-305). After sailing for four days, the ship carrying Felix arrived at Agrigentum in Sicily. There the local Christians met and prayed with the prisoner-bishop. After returning to the ship, Felix journeyed to Vernosa in Apulia. There the prefect asked Felix if he had the sacred texts and if he would hand them over. Felix responded in the affirmative to the first question and in the negative to the second. The prefect then ordered that Felix immediately be beheaded.

Scholars report, "The story of the deportation of St. Felix to Italy and his martyrdom there is no more than a hagiographer's fiction to make him an Italian saint: there seems no doubt at all that he suffered at Carthage by order of the proconsul there, and his relics were subsequently laid to rest in the well-known *basilica Fausti* in that city."[11]

30 ✢ St. Marcellus

Place: *Tingis in Mauretania (now Tangier in Morocco)*
Fame: *Christian centurion who refused to worship Roman gods*

While encamped at Tingis, soldiers of the Roman army were celebrating the anniversary of Emperor Maximian (r. 286-305), when the centurion Marcellus not only refused to participate in the pagan festivities but also threw down his soldier's belt and insignia in front of the legion's standards. He shouted, "I serve the eternal king, Jesus. Henceforth I will not serve your emperors, and I disdain to worship your gods, deaf and dumb idols made of wood and stone."[12] Immediately the nearby soldiers surrounded Marcellus, took him into custody, and held him in confinement until the celebrations were concluded. The prisoner was then brought before Fortunatus, the president of the assembly.

Fortunatus questioned Marcellus as to his reason for his apparently rash behavior. The Christian explained that he could not offer worship to the emperor but only to Jesus Christ. Fortunatus replied, "I cannot overlook your reckless behavior, and accordingly I shall report this matter to the emperors and the caesar. You will be sent to my lord Aurelius Agricolanus, deputy of the praetorian prefect."[13] Two months later, Agricolanus interrogated Marcellus. The following dialogue is regarded as original and genuine.

Agricolanus: "What madness possessed you to throw away the badges of your allegiance and to speak as you did?"

Marcellus: "There is no madness in those who fear God."

Agricolanus: "Did you say each of the things that are contained in the president's report?"

Marcellus: "I did."

Agricolanus: "Did you cast away your arms?"

Marcellus: "I did. For it was not right for a Christian, who serves the Lord Christ, to serve in the armies of the world."

Agricolanus: "Discipline requires that what Marcellus has done should be punished." And he pronounced sentence: "Marcellus, who held the rank of regular centurion, has admitted that he degraded himself by openly repudiating his allegiance, and furthermore said other insane things, as related in the official report: it is therefore our pleasure that he be put to death by the sword."[14]

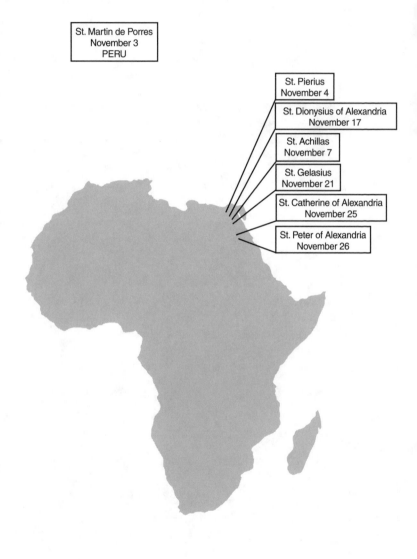

NOVEMBER

3 ✢ St. Martin de Porres

Place: Lima, Peru

Fame: Humble service, recipient of extraordinary
spiritual phenomena

Martin (1579-1639) "inherited the features and dark complex-
ion of his mother,"[1] Anna Velasquez, who was a freed slave for-
merly from Panama. His father, Juan de Porres, was a Spanish
nobleman and knight of Alcántara, who was initially embar-
rassed by Martin's color. Because the father refused to admit
paternity, Martin's baptismal record reads, "Martin, son of an
unknown father."[2] The father abandoned the family when
Martin and his younger sister, Juana, were toddlers. When Martin was eight years old, the father returned and took his son and
daughter to Guayaquil, Ecuador, where he had been appointed
governor. Martin's parents never married.

When Martin was twelve, the father returned to Lima and
arranged for Martin to be apprenticed to a barber-surgeon. These
practitioners, according to the custom of the day, not only cut
hair but also bound medical wounds, let blood, and dispensed
medicines. The position entailed serving as "a barber, surgeon,
doctor and pharmacist."[3] After approximately three years in this
career, Martin requested admission to the Dominican Order as a
lay helper. He wished to perform for the monks the menial tasks
of sweeping corridors and cleaning toilets. Martin's father had
hoped that his son might become a priest or at least a lay brother.
Martin, however, refused any prompting by his father. Martin
sought the lowest of positions. He quoted Psalm 84: "I would

rather be a doorkeeper in the house of my God than live in the tents of wickedness."[4] He lived in a storage room, ate sparingly, slept on a bed of planks, attended numerous Masses each morning, and received Holy Communion on all Sundays and major feasts of Our Lord and his Blessed Mother.

Martin's dedication to God and the religious life impressed the members of his Dominican religious community. After serving as a lay helper for nine years, Martin was urged by the community's leaders, in 1594, to take vows as a lay brother. The humble servant relented and accepted the invitation. His tasks at the monastery remained simple: answering the door for visitors, maintaining the linen closet, caring for the medical needs of the monks, and distributing bread to hungry beggars. Priests and lay members of the monastery sought out this holy lay brother for spiritual guidance. Even the novice director sought Martin's assistance in guiding the spiritual lives of the young candidates. In his free time, Martin ministered outside the monastery, founding an orphanage, visiting the sick and dying in the community, visiting criminals in prisons, and caring for African slaves at the New World's busiest port of Lima. "This half-Spanish, half-Negro Peruvian loved all men without regard to race, color, or station, and he served Christ in all men without measuring the cost."[5]

Martin practiced prayer and penance to an unusual degree. The inspiration for his life and labors was the suffering servant Jesus. Someone peering through the keyhole in the door to his room spied on him at prayer: "On his knees motionless, his face bathed in tears, his arms outstretched in the form of a cross, his eyes fixed on the crucifix, Martin seemed to have concentrated his whole being in that gaze and that posture which reflected the object of his contemplation."[6] Martin experienced spiritual phenomena virtually unparalleled among the saints of the Church. "The extraordinary was ordinary in Martin de Porres's life: visions, ecstasies, terrifying penances, bilocation, infused theological knowledge, miraculous cures and astonishing control over animals."[7] Added to that list are aerial flight, knowledge of the future, confrontations with the devil, plus the ability to walk through walls and locked gates. The stories are astounding in their kind and number.

Interestingly, four other persons whom the Church later would canonize as saints lived at Lima at that same time. Rose of Lima lived one block away from the Dominican monastery, and every day for many years she visited Martin before she eventually became a Dominican tertiary. Archbishop Turibius Mongrovejo taught both Martin and Rose in the same confirmation class. Another lay brother, John Massias, lived in the Dominican monastery located right next door to Martin's. Francis Solano, the fiery Franciscan preacher who wore out his welcome in Spain, found a new home at Lima in the New World. "Martin was in good company, surrounded by so many privileged souls who aspired to the heights of perfection."[8] One wonders about the mutual benefit these saints enjoyed. Specifically, one wonders about the inspiration that Martin received and gave in living the Christian life.

4 ✠ St. Pierius

Place: *Alexandria, Egypt*
Fame: *Scholarly and saintly head of the catechetical school*

The priest Pierius (d.c. 310) was associated with, but needs to be distinguished from, his contemporary and controversial colleague Origen. Because Pierius was taught by Origen at the renowned catechetical school at Alexandria, Pierius perceived himself as a disciple of Origen. The young priest was oftentimes referred to as the "younger Origen." In time, Pierius became head of the same famed school where he taught St. Pamphilus, who later defended Origen.

While some scholars have discovered a similarity in thought between Pierius and Origen, it is important to note that Pierius, unlike Origen, never aroused the wrath of his bishop. Origen had preached before being ordained, had accepted ordination outside of his bishop's diocese without his bishop's approval, and had castrated himself in literal response to the Gospel mandate, "If your right eye causes you to sin, tear it out and throw it away. . . . If your hand causes you to sin, cut it off and throw it away."[9] Pierius did none of these things for which Origen was criticized.

"Pierius was a noted exegete, preacher, and ascetic."[10] He won renown for his theological and philosophical learning and labors. Numerous scholars, notably St. Jerome, Eusebius, and Philip Sedetes, praised the saintly scholar. Pierius suffered during the persecution of Diocletian (r. 284–305) but survived and eventually died at Rome. Centuries later, "Photius," the patriarch of Constantinople and leader of the Byzantine intellectual renaissance, "speaks of his (Pierius') temperance and poverty, and the clear, brilliant and spontaneous qualities of his writings."[11]

7 ✣ St. Achillas

Place: Alexandria, Egypt
Fame: He ordained Arius but later criticized him
for his heretical teachings

Achillas (d. 313) was ordained bishop of Alexandria in 311, when he was already a very old man. His episcopacy lasted only a few months, from late in 311 until mid-June of 312. The episcopacy at Alexandria was no easy assignment for the elderly bishop. Alexandria was the second most populous city in the Roman Empire. The city's million-plus population lived at the crossroads of culture and commerce, where ideas from the East and West and South were daily exchanged. Part of the responsibility of being named bishop of Alexandria was to be named at the same time the director of that city's famous catechetical school.

One idea that became popular at Alexandria and flourished far beyond Egypt was the teaching that Jesus was not equal with God the Father but secondary in time and nature to him. It was taught that Jesus was human but not divine. The major proponent of this idea was Arius.

Achillas is remembered especially for his having ordained Arius a priest. In ordaining Arius, Bishop Achillas advanced to the altar one of the Catholic Church's most nefarious heretics. Later, when Achillas realized the unorthodox theology of Arius, the bishop challenged the priest. It was, however, too late. The seeds of the heresy had been planted. Arius then attacked Achillas. The Meletians joined in the attack against the bishop. Achillas became broken in heart and in health.

Achillas's episcopal successors Alexander and his secretary Athanasius became successive bishops of Alexandria and the Church's most prominent opponents of Arius and his teachings. After Achillas had died, Alexander convened in 320 a council that condemned Arius. The condemned priest fled then to Palestine, where he continued teaching that Jesus was an exemplary man but not the Incarnate Son of God.

17 ✞ St. Dionysius of Alexandria

Place: *Alexandria, Egypt*
Fame: *Father of the Church and archbishop*

In his native Alexandria, Dionysius (c. 190–265) studied literature and philosophy. He converted to Christianity in his youth.

At the catechetical school, he was taught by Origen and, in 232, became head of that school. Fifteen years later, he was ordained bishop of Alexandria.

During the persecution instigated by Decius (r. 249–251), Dionysius was arrested, but he escaped and went into hiding in the Libyan desert in 250. One year later, when the anti-Christian action ended, the bishop returned to the capital city. The brief respite ended when the persecution under Valerian (r. 253–260) arose in 257. This time, rather than flee and hide as before, Dionysius publicly professed his faith. For this display, he was exiled to Libya. Three years later, when he returned to the capital, he found a social structure rapidly deteriorating under the weight of civil war. The bishop dedicated his remaining years to caring physically and spiritually for the victims of civil war and religious persecution.

The archbishop involved himself in the major theological disputes of the day: the various Trinitarian heresies, plus Novatianism, Chilianism, and the rebaptism controversy. Pope St. Cornelius appreciated Dionysius' support against the usurping antipope Novatian. The next two popes, however, rebuked Dionysius for his positions: St. Stephen on account of Dionysius' support of Cyprian in the controversy surrounding the rebaptism of heretics, and St. Dionysius because of the Alexandrian Dionysius' questionable views on the Trinity.

The writings of this Father of the Church remain extant only in fragmentary form: a book *On Nature* plus tracts in which he denied the Johannine authorship of both the Apocalypse and two of the three letters ascribed to John.[12]

21 ✣ St. Gelasius

Place: Vandal kingdom of Africa
(now in Algeria, Tunisia, and Libya)
Fame: Pope from 492 to 496

The most ancient source available states that Gelasius (d. 496) was an "African by birth, whose father was Valerius."[13] Other reputable but not so ancient sources claim that Gelasius' father was African and that Gelasius himself was born at Rome. The dispute continues whether this pope was African-born or of African descent.

Undisputed is the significance of Gelasius' contribution. One author writes, "Gelasius is one of the remarkable popes in the first centuries of the Church, but he is largely unknown because of the greater fame and renown of Pope St. Leo I."[14] Another commentator adds, "Next to Leo I, Gelasius was the outstanding pope of the fifth century, and he surpassed Leo in theological grasp."[15] Both Leo and Gelasius, as well as the dozen other popes of that century, contended against threats to the Roman papacy at a time when the Roman Empire was collapsing. The responses made by Leo and Gelasius continue to make an impact even today.

> If Leo I can be said to have laid the juridical foundations of papal authority for all time, Gelasius I applied those principles in letters that read very much like legal briefs. There was little that subsequent generations could add to his explicit statements about papal supremacy or the relations between Church and State, except a spelling out of what was contained in his thought.[16]

Gelasius inherited the Acacian Schism from his predecessor, Felix II. Gelasius had served as Felix's archdeacon and possibly composed Felix's correspondence in this case. Felix excommunicated Patriarch Acacius of Constantinople in 484 because he had appointed bishops to some Eastern sees without first seeking and receiving approval from Rome. To add insult to injury, it was discovered later that these bishops had Monophysite leanings. This theological dispute carried with it political ramifications because Patriarch Acacius had acted in collusion with Emperor Zeno (r. 474-491). Even after Acacius and Zeno died, Gelasius refused to accept the olive branch offered by Constantinople to Rome until Acacius' successor eliminated his predecessor's name from the Eastern Church's public lists of revered deceased. This intransigence by Rome drew not only resentment from the Eastern emperor and ecclesiastics but also murmurings from members of the Western clergy. Tensions arose. When the new emperor refused to remove Acacius' name, Gelasius sent to the political leader Gelasius' theory on the relation between Church and State. Gelasius taught that both institutions receive authority from God to act independently within their legitimate jurisdiction, but that in a situation of mixed jurisdiction, sacred authority inherently exceeds that of secular authority. This viewpoint reached its fullest development in the medieval model of Church-State relations.

A Roman synod that was held the year before Gelasius died "is remembered as the first-known occasion when the Pope was hailed as the Vicar of Christ."[17] That synod helped to oppose successfully a Roman senator's efforts to restore the pagan feast of Lupercalia and warned against a resurgence of Pelagianism in the Adriatic regions of Picenum on the west coast and Dalmatia on the east coast. A synod held the previous year had affirmed Gelasius' decree that revenue which accrued from Church property would be distributed for four purposes: the poor, the clergy, the bishop, and the maintenance of church buildings; this decree still applies to sees under the metropolitan jurisdiction of Rome.

Gelasius wrote prolifically. Eighteen of his Mass formularies are preserved in the Leonine Sacramentary and slightly more than one hundred of his letters in whole or in part remain extant. Although traditionally the Gelasian Sacramentary and the Decretum of canonical Scriptures have been attributed to him, scholars today suggest that this pope did not author those two works but rather created the Gelasian Renaissance that gave rise to those works. He did teach that the Eucharist must be consumed under two species in order to counter the Manichaeans, who taught that wine was impure and should not be drunk.

Administratively, Gelasius achieved what he did at the same time that the Western empire was being overrun by the barbarians. Gelasius befriended the Ostrogoth king Theodoric (r. 487-493), who had conquered the entire territory of Italy, and persuaded him to remain neutral during the Catholic Church's East-West disputes. Without his neutrality, Theodoric could have sabotaged Gelasius' efforts by adding internal politico-military unrest to his politico-religious problems. Instead, Theodoric conducted himself as a respected friend. The pope even succeeded in having the barbarian contribute funds to the relief effort for the war-torn population. The pope himself already had set the example by distributing to the needy both his private wealth and papal revenues. Pope Gelasius, who was born wealthy, died penniless. Because of the civil chaos that enveloped Rome and the surrounding regions, few persons could be freed to prepare for the priesthood. Gelasius responded by relaxing the standards in order that people might have priests.

Gelasius' public persona is oftentimes that of being intransigent, but the Church benefited from his far-reaching vision and fortitude under fire. His private persona, enjoyed by those who met and worked with him, is that of an exceptionally prayerful and generous servant.

25 ✛ St. Catherine of Alexandria

Place: Alexandria, Egypt
Fame: Alleged martyr

The details of Catherine (d.c. 310) come from two sources, neither of which has significant historical veracity.

The story of her conversion informs readers that Catherine was born at Alexandria to a wealthy family. She received a vision of Christ that led to her immediate baptism and lifelong mystical union with Jesus. Allegedly, she publicly denounced to his face Emperor Maxentius (r. 306–312) for his persecution of Christians. Many of those in attendance, hearing her and witnessing her courage, converted, including fifty pagan philosophers. The emperor had the converts killed. To Catherine, however, he offered to preserve her life if she would agree to a royal marriage. Maxentius jailed the patrician woman while he went out on a review of his troops.

Upon his return home, the emperor discovered that Catherine had been busy converting the empress, an officer, and two hundred soldiers. Again, Maxentius killed the converts. He ordered soldiers to lay out Catherine's body alive on a spiked wheel, and then to stretch and press her body to death. In the process of applying the torture, however, the wheel of death broke. The emperor ordered that Catherine simply be beheaded.

It seems that the remains of Catherine's body were retrieved and carried to the monastery of St. Catherine at Mount Sinai, where the monastery and supposed relics remain today in the Sinai Peninsula. "The earliest evidence of her cult, apparently introduced by Eastern monks who had fled from iconoclasm, appears in a painting of the early eighth century in Rome. After the tenth century, her cult became very popular, especially in Italy."[18] Five centuries later, St. Joan of Arc claimed that she heard the voice of St. Catherine. In 1969, however, the Roman Catholic Church officially removed the cult of Catherine from the Church's liturgical calendar because of lack of evidence of her having been a real historical figure.

26 ✠ St. Peter of Alexandria

Place: *Alexandria, Egypt*
Fame: *Last martyr of the Roman persecution at Alexandria*

Having come to episcopal office in 300, Peter (d. 311) endured from 303 until his martyrdom in 311 the effects of the persecution initiated by Diocletian (r. 284-305) and continued by his successors, especially Maximian (r. 286-305) in the West and Galerius (r. 305-311) in the East. Peter, a highly educated and inspiring former head of the catechetical school at Alexandria, spent his time as bishop preaching, teaching, and writing to members of his Catholic flock. He consoled those who were about to die for the faith. Those who had not yet been arrested, he encouraged to keep the faith despite its risks. And those who had denied the faith by having handed over the Church's Scriptures or sacred vessels, he received back compassionately into the Church. "St. Peter published fourteen canons of instruction as to how such *lapsi* who wished to be reconciled were to be treated, and these canons were later adopted by the whole Eastern church."[19]

Eventually, the Roman authorities came looking for Peter to arrest him. He fled to the desert. In the patriarch's absence, Meletius, the bishop of Lycopolis, usurped the authority of Peter and ordained men for Peter's diocese. Meletius performed similarly illicit ordinations in other dioceses where the local bishops were assigned but absent because they were in hiding. Meletius added insult to injury by criticizing Peter for two kinds of weakness: running from danger and receiving back too quickly those who had lapsed. Communicating from the desert, Peter begged Meletius to desist from his destructive activity. Meletius refused. Peter responded by excommunicating the usurper.

When a temporary lull occurred in the persecution, Peter returned to the capital city. Unfortunately, a new administration gave rise to a new persecution. Maximianus (r. 286–305) took up in the West where Diocletian (r. 284–305) had left off in the East. Roman authorities seized the bishop. Without making a charge and without holding a trial, the Roman authorities whisked Peter away and executed him. "In Egypt St. Peter is called the 'Seal and Complement of the Persecution' because he was the last martyr put to death by public authority at Alexandria."[20]

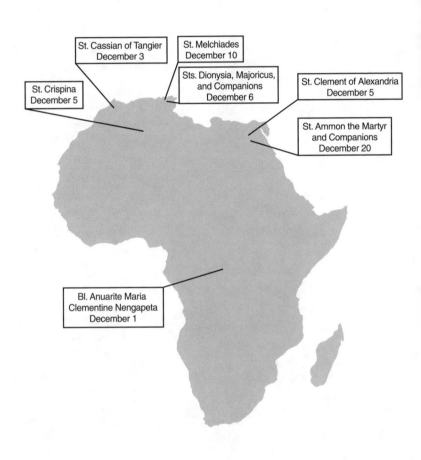

DECEMBER

1 ✣ Bl. Anuarite Maria Clementine Nengapeta

Place: *Matali, Congo (now in Zaire)*
Fame: *Nun martyred for her virginity*

Although not born into a Christian family, Anuarite (1939-1964) along with her mother and sisters sought and received baptism in 1943. As a young girl, Anuarite felt an inclination toward the spiritual life. At fifteen, she entered the convent of the Sisters of the Holy Family at Bafwabaka. There she took as her religious name Maria Clementine. Five years later, she took the religious vows of chastity, poverty, and obedience. By her daily demonstration of faith, hope, and love, she earned among her fellow sisters the reputation of being a genuine "servant of the Lord."[1] She did all that she did for the love of Christ.

Ever since the natives had declared the political independence of the Belgian Congo (now Zaire) in 1960, the nation experienced sporadic politico-military turmoil. During one of those periods, when the military was usurping the prominence and power rightfully reserved for political leaders, Anuarite literally crossed the path of a military parade. A colonel named Olombe called for the young nun to come to him. When she responded, the colonel made sexual advances. Anuarite refused to succumb to the harassment. Angered that the young nun rejected him, the colonel killed her on the spot. The whole country immediately recognized her as a martyr in defense of sexual purity.[2]

3 ✠ St. Cassian of Tangier

Place: Tingis, Mauretania (now Tangier in Morocco)
Fame: Martyr for justice

The judge Aurelius Agricolan decreed the death sentence for both the Roman soldier Marcellus and the local court clerk Cassian (d. 298) for their adherence to the Christian faith. While Church historians and hagiographers have agreed that both men suffered capital punishment, scholars have disagreed about the details of the events.

The context of the story is that the centurion Marcellus was being tried in court on the charge of being a Christian and that the court stenographer Cassian was recording the dialogue. When the judge condemned Marcellus to death for being a Christian, Cassian immediately and conspicuously threw down his stylus. The judge asked for an explanation of the outburst in the courtroom. Cassian replied that the sentence was unjust. With that, both the defendant and the clerk were led away: Marcellus to be beheaded immediately and Cassian to be jailed until his trial could be arranged.

On December 3, some weeks after Marcellus's beheading on the previous October 30, Cassian was led back into the same courtroom where Marcellus's trial had taken place. A similar series of questions and answers occurred. Similar, too, was the outcome: Cassian was led away and beheaded.

5 ✛ St. Clement of Alexandria

Place: Alexandria, Egypt
Fame: Teacher of Origen and Father of the Church

Like his predecessor St. Pantaenus, Clement (d.c. 217) directed the catechetical school at Alexandria and taught Origen. During the persecution of Emperor Septimus Severus, Clement fled Egypt and sought shelter in Asia Minor. The classically educated scholar never returned to Alexandria and died fifteen years later at Cappadocia, near his friend Alexander, bishop of Constantinople, who later became bishop of Jerusalem. Some modern scholars question whether Clement was born in Africa or taught Origen. Some sources do not include Clement in their encyclopedic lists of saints.

Clement was a prolific author. He weaves Gnosticism, Stoicism, and Platonism in a tapestry to support Christianity. He takes from these philosophical schools whatever is useful to and coincides with Christian spirituality, morality, and theology. Never does he succumb to unorthodoxy; always he explains the Church's teachings in a way that is faithful to the Scriptures and tradition. "In Christian thought he opened an optimistic and liberal approach to secular knowledge, laying the foundations for a Christian humanism and introducing philosophy to its role as 'the servant of theology.' "[3]

> Clement was a cultured Greek philosopher and scholar, though his erudition was often secondhand; a Christian apologist and exegete; a theologian and mystic. His open mind and enthusiasm are reflected in a varied literary output, original and daring in content, refined and elegant in style. The absence of method and synthesis in his work was often calculated, but it disconcerts the modern reader.[4]

5 ✛ St. Crispina

Place: Theveste, Numidia (now in Algeria)
Fame: Martyred in the last Roman persecution

In an all-out effort to unify the empire by imposing pagan religious unity, the emperor Diocletian (r. 284-305) wielded a particularly cruel and extensive persecution. In Numidia at that time, the noblewoman Crispina (d. 304), who had come from great wealth and had borne many children, defied the proconsul Anulinus and defended her Christian faith.

When the proconsul read to her the imperial edict requiring sacrifices to the pagan gods, Crispina replied, "I have never sacrificed and I shall not do so save to the one true God and to our Lord, Jesus Christ, his Son, who was born and died."[5] Repeatedly the proconsul appealed to her to offer incense, to give up what he perceived as superstition, stupidity, and stubbornness on her part. Repeatedly, she refused. In her answers, she teased the clerk by saying that she would obey, but then clarified her answer, "I will obey the edict, but the one given by my Lord Jesus Christ."[6] Anulinus tried to frighten her by threatening to behead her, to shave off her hair and parade her publicly. She replied, "That religion is worthless . . . which forces men to be crushed against their will. . . . I do not fear anything you say."[7]

Anulinus interrupted Crispina. He tried to reason with her: "Do you wish to live a long time or die in agony like so many of your companions?"[8] She answered, "If I wished to die and give my soul to destruction in the eternal fire, I should already have surrendered my will to your demons."[9] The proconsul briefly continued the proceedings, then concluded, "Seeing that Crispina has persisted in infamous superstition and refuses to offer sacrifice to our gods in accordance with the heavenly decrees of the Augustan law, I have ordered her to be executed with the sword."[10] With the verdict having been decreed, Crispina replied, " 'I bless God who has so deigned to free me from your hands. Thanks be to God!' And making the sign of the cross on her forehead and putting out her neck, she was beheaded in the name of the Lord Jesus Christ, to whom is honour for ever."[11]

6 ✣ Sts. Dionysia, Majoricus, and Companions

Place: Byzacena (now in Tunisia)
Fame: Cruelly tortured by the Vandals

At a time when those bishops who had not yet been sent into exile, he (Huneric) sent simultaneously through all the provinces of the land of Africa most cruel torturers, so that there did not remain a single home or place free of wailing and lamentations. They did not spare people of any age or either sex, except those who submitted to their will. Some were tortured by being beaten, others by being hung, and others by the fire; contrary to the laws of nature, women, especially the noble, were tortured entirely naked and in full view of the public.[12]

Dionysia (d. 484) suffered in the above-mentioned fashion. Stripped, beaten, and positioned in a prominent place, she shouted to her tormentors, "You servants of the Devil, what you think you are doing to my shame is in fact to my praise."[13] Spotting in the crowd her anguished son Majoricus (d. 484), she shot him glances that his eyes saw and his heart felt. When the son was brought forth for torture, she spoke to him, "The punishment to be feared is the one which will never end, and the life to be desired is the one which will be enjoyed for ever."[14]

Many other persons suffered along with the above-mentioned mother and son: her sister, Dativa; her cousin, Emilian, who was a physician; Leonitia, the daughter of the bishop Germanus; Tertius, who was renowned for his strong faith; and Boniface of Sibida and Servus of Tuburbo, who had suffered under Genseric (r. 428–477) and again under Huneric (r. 477–484). Beatings, hangings from pulleys and being quickly dropped to the pavement, and skin-tearing draggings behind horses racing through the city were among the cruel tortures Christians suffered for their faith.

10 ✛ St. Melchiades

Place: *Proconsular Africa (now in Algeria, Tunisia, and Libya)*
Fame: *Pope from 311 to 314*

In his brief tenure, Pope Melchiades (d. 314), also called Miltiades, witnessed the fortuitous cessation of the anti-Christian persecution at Rome and the unfortunate birth of the Donatist heresy in Africa. The most ancient source describes Melchiades as probably African in origin, whereas later sources dispute this information and claim that Melchiades was probably of Roman origin and of African descent.[15]

After a one-year to three-year vacancy of the papacy, Melchiades was elected pope. He benefited immediately from Emperor Maxentius' (r. 306-312) Edict of Toleration, which had been promulgated just one month before Melchiades ascended to the papacy. All Church lands, buildings, and sacred vessels that had been confiscated during the Diocletian (r. 284-305) persecution, which had begun in 303, were now to be returned to Church ownership. One year later, this same Maxentius was defeated when Constantine (r. 307-337) victoriously crossed the Tiber River at the Milvian Bridge. Upon victoriously entering the city of Rome, the new emperor in the West along with his co-emperor in the East, Licinius (r. 308-324), declared the Edict of Milan (313), whereby all religions, including Christianity, were to be tolerated. The new emperor then gave Empress Faustus's residence, known as the Lateran Palace, to the pope. This Lateran Palace became and remained the papal residence for a millennium until the Avignon Papacy.

Melchiades had little opportunity to enjoy the happy turn of events in Rome because of the contentious situation in Africa. Theological rigorists there had objected in 311 to the election of Caecilian as bishop of Carthage. They charged that one of the bishops who had ordained Caecilian had handed over the Church's sacred texts to the government during a previous persecution. The ordinations conferred by him, including the ordination of Caecilian, were invalid. Donatus and his disciples had claimed that the holiness of the minister is necessary to make valid the Church's sacraments; moreover, they insisted, laity and clergy who had lapsed during persecution needed to be rebaptized and, where applicable, reordained. Having rejected Caecilian, the rigorists elected Majorinus as their bishop. He soon died and the rigorists elected Donatus to take his place. This controversy, while theological in origin, gained popular support because it pitted the native Berber population against the foreign-oriented Romans, and the laboring class against the landowners. The rigorists appealed to Emperor Constantine to hear and decide their case.

Constantine asked Pope Melchiades and three bishops from Gaul to submit a joint recommendation to the emperor on this matter. Melchiades's first action was to change the composition and purpose of the commission. First, he expanded the emperor's committee of four persons by adding another fifteen bishops of his own choosing. Second, rather than propose a recommendation to the emperor, the pope transformed the political committee into an ecclesiastical synod with authority to make its own decisions. The synod, which met at the Lateran Palace, upheld the election of Caecilian. This decision concurred with Roman Catholic theology that the effectiveness of a sacrament does not depend on the worthiness of the minister. The synod also excommunicated Donatus. Politically, Melchiades isolated Donatus by promising the African bishops who had been supporting Donatus that if they would vote with the pope, the pope would permit these bishops to return to full union with the Church and to retain their ecclesiastical positions. The African bishops yielded to Melchiades's theological position and ecclesiastical power.

Melchiades's decision and his manipulation of the process enraged the Donatists. They appealed a second, then a third, time to the emperor who, in return, convened councils at Arles in 314 and at Milan in 316. Both councils came to the same decision as had Melchiades's council at Rome in 313. "It is significant that the emperor, in calling the council (at Arles), did not regard the pope's decision as final and that neither Melchiades nor his successor took exception to the emperor's actions."[16] Melchiades, who had died in January 314, escaped further involvement in this controversy. Donatism survived until 439, when the Vandals vanquished not only the Donatists but also the Catholic faith in the proconsular province of Africa.

20 ✠ St. Ammon the Martyr and Companions

Place: Egypt, Alexandria
Fame: Christian soldiers who died in support of Christian prisoners

Dionysius, the bishop of Alexandria, wrote to Fabian, the bishop of Antioch, in Syria, about the tragic but heroic situations of

Christians having been persecuted in his see during the reign of the Emperor Decius (r. 249-251). In one incident, a Christian prisoner who was facing martyrdom showed signs of wavering in his faith. Some soldiers responded by encouraging the man. "Some Christian soldiers who were among the guards, fearing that the man would deny his faith, made signs to him by looks, gestures and nods to stand firm."[17] When the magistrate observed the encouragement that some of the government's own soldiers were offering, he ordered them to desist and to step forward. Several soldiers — Ammon (d. 250), Ingenes, Ptolemy, and Zeno — and an older man, Theophilus, advanced and declared their faith. All the soldiers were beheaded on the spot.

A BRIEF HISTORY
OF THE CATHOLIC CHURCH
IN AFRICA

I. The first seven hundred years: the origin, expansion, and decline of the Church in North Africa.

The Apostolic Age (first century) ‡ The New Testament and Church tradition identify numerous saintly persons who either originated from Africa or visited there.

The Holy Family fled to Egypt to escape the wrath of Herod, the paranoid Roman-appointed king of Judea. The Gospel reports, "Now when they [the wise men] had departed, behold, an angel of the Lord appeared to Joseph in a dream and said, 'Rise, take the child and his mother, and flee to Egypt, and remain there until I tell you; for Herod is about to search for the child, to destroy him.' "[1] Father, mother, and child fled to what traditionally is believed to be Heliopolis. The flight "was to fulfil what the Lord had spoken by the prophet, 'Out of Egypt have I called my son.' "[2]

Egypt, Cyrene, and Ethiopia are mentioned in the scriptural stories of the last days of Jesus and the first days of the spread of the Church. The "devout Jews from every nation" who were staying in Jerusalem and heard the apostles speaking in the visitors' tongues included Jews from "Egypt, and the parts of Libya belonging to Cyrene."[3] Simon of Cyrene was taken from the crowd to assist Jesus in carrying his cross.[4] At Antioch, Lucius of Cyrene was among the handful of teachers and prophets from whom the Spirit called Barnabas and Paul to serve as missionaries among the Diaspora Jews and Gentiles.[5] The apostle Philip, while traveling on the desert route from Jerusalem down to Gaza, was directed by the Spirit to approach a fellow traveler, an Ethiopian eunuch who was a court official and overseer of the treasury of his country's queen, Candace. Philip instructed the eunuch and the man asked to be baptized.[6]

Both St. Luke and St. Paul write favorably about Apollos of Alexandria. Luke presents Apollos as "an eloquent man, well versed in the scriptures, . . . [who] spoke with burning enthusiasm and taught accurately the things concerning Jesus."[7] Apollos, it seems, had been baptized by John the Baptist but never received the baptism of the Holy Spirit, until at Ephesus. Priscilla and Aquila "took him aside and explained the Way of God to him more accurately."[8] The Alexandrian later traveled to Corinth, where he was evangelizing at the same time that Paul was rejoicing over the many converts won by Apollos at Ephesus. Returning to Corinth, Paul discovered that cliques had formed around the various preachers of the Gospel: Peter, Paul, and Apollos. Paul urged the Corinthians not to focus on the messengers but on the message: "Let no one boast about human leaders. . . . All things are yours, whether Paul or Apollos, or Cephas, . . . you belong to Christ, and Christ belongs to God."[9] Paul described Apollos and himself as "God's servants" and requested Titus to send Apollos from Crete to continue the ministry of the Gospel at Corinth.[10]

According to tradition, St. Mark the evangelist came to Egypt, where he served as the country's first Christian missionary and first bishop of Alexandria. This tradition is recorded as early as the fourth century by both Eusebius, in his *Ecclesiastical History*, and St. Jerome, in the preface of the Latin Vulgate edition of the Gospels. Mark is remembered as the fleet-footed youth who ran away practically naked after he had overheard Jewish leaders at Jerusalem plotting to kill Jesus, as the resident of the home to which St. Peter fled upon his angel-effected escape from prison, and as the missionary who evangelized with

Barnabas and Paul at Syria, Crete, and Pamphylia.[11] Mark became reconciled with Paul and honored his request to visit Rome to assist the apostle of the Gentiles.[12] Mark assisted St. Peter, who affectionately calls the young disciple "my son Mark."[13] Churchmen from the second to the fourth centuries, namely St. Clement of Alexandria, St. Irenaeus, Origen, and Papias, all refer to Mark as "the disciple and interpreter of St. Peter."[14] This is the background and reputation of St. Mark, who tradition teaches evangelized at Egypt.

The Growth of Christianity (second and third centuries) ✠
Martyrdom and monasticism led to the rapid growth of the native Church and the intellectual development of the faith.

For almost a century and a half, from 180 to 311, Christians in Africa suffered intermittent waves of imperial persecution. Personal and Church properties were confiscated. People of every age and sex were tortured, exiled, or killed on account of their faith. One of the earliest instances of Christian martyrdom ever recorded occurred in 180 at Carthage, where Speratus and eleven companions from the town of Scillium refused the proconsul's order to offer sacrifice to the emperor. For this defiance against paganism and defense of Christianity the dozen persons were beheaded. Two decades later in the same city, the young mothers Perpetua and Felicity, along with three Christian men, were thrown into the amphitheater, where wild animals mauled the men to death and where gladiators, in response to the audience's directions, killed the women. Half a century later and thirty miles to the west at Utica, the governor ordered numerous Christians to choose between offering incense to the gods and being thrown into a white-hot limekiln. The Christians did not wait to be thrown into the fire; instead, they jumped in. A few hundred miles to the east at Alexandria, which was suffering the effects of Roman civil war and citywide violence, it was the Christians who gladly gave up their lives in caring for plague victims. Far removed from Africa, at a battle site on the Rhône River in the Swiss Alps, a legion of Egyptian Christian soldiers from Thebes refused to invoke the protection of the Roman gods before a battle. The emperor's envoy listened to the Christians' explanation and then repeated the order: worship Roman gods or be killed. This happened in 287, when Maurice and countless members of the legion were slaughtered.

The greatest persecution began around 297, became general in 303, and lasted until 311, when the elderly and infirm emperor Diocletian retired from political office to his country villa. At Numidia, a young man named Maximilian refused to be a soldier for the emperor because he had dedicated his life to be a soldier for Christ. Maximilian lost his life on account of this profession of faith. These persecutions were directed toward people of all religions, including Christianity, to foster political unity through religious unity; the order to offer sacrifice "was conceived as an oath of allegiance to the emperor and the Roman state."[15] These persecutions were mandated for particular places prior to 250 and for the entire empire from 250 until 311, although the order was implemented to varying degrees in various places. Only a few of the more than forty emperors who ruled from 180 to 311 mandated persecutions: notably, prior to 250, Marcus Aurelius, Commodus, and Septimus Severus; from 250 onward, Decius, Valerian, Gallienus, and Diocletian. Diocletian applied persecution in an especially thorough way.

Most emperors of the third century had promoted the worship of the sun as a unifying theme, a cult which few of their subjects would have difficulty in accepting. Diocletian instead went back to the traditional Roman gods such as Jove and Hercules. This was to have dire consequences for the Christians, who by now formed a large minority group within the army and the imperial administration. The first blow fell in 297 or 298, when Diocletian issued an order requiring all soldiers and administrators to sacrifice to the gods; those who refused were forced to quit the service. So matters stood for six years. Then on 24 February 303, an edict was issued ordering the destruction of churches and scriptures throughout the empire, and the punishment of leading Christians. Further edicts later that same year ordered the arrest and imprisonment of the entire Christian clergy; they were to be released only after they had sacrificed to the traditional gods. In April 304, a final edict commanded all Christians, clergy and laity alike, to offer sacrifice, on pain of death.[16]

Tertullian, the great African Christian apologist, provides the immortal phrase: "The blood of martyrs is the seed of Christians." Despite the bloodshed, the universal Church grew enormously. In Africa, by 225, at least seventy bishops oversaw dioceses in Numidia and proconsular Africa, and shortly thereafter, another seventy bishops served in Egypt. By the time Augustine was appointed bishop of Hippo in 396, over three hundred bishops were serving in Africa, not including the bishops serving in Egypt. Approximately one third of the more than one million population of Egypt's capital city were said to have been Christians.

Martyrdom led to monasticism. During the Decian persecution from 250 to 251, some Christians from the city of Thebes in Upper Egypt fled to the surrounding deserts. Paul the First Hermit (c. 229–c. 342) and others like him lived the solitary life there. When Antony (251–356) moved from the city of Memphis to the neighboring desert, so many hermits kept joining him that he kept moving farther and farther out into the desert, eventually to Colzim in 272.

Intense theological discussions took place at this time. Two highly educated converts from paganism to Christianity highlighted the Church's intellectual activity: Tertullian (c. 160–220) and St. Cyprian (c. 200–258). Tertullian defended the faith against pagans and the heretics of Montanism and Manichaeanism. This great apologist was a genius at one-liners; he "is the most quotable of all ancient Christian writers, . . . he had a gift for the phrase rather than the paragraph."[17] Cyprian, the bishop of Carthage, corresponded with three popes. The first, Cornelius, praised the bishop for upholding the need that the *lapsi* do penance as a condition for being reinstated in the Church. The second, Stephen, threatened Cyprian with excommunication for insisting on the rebaptism of heretics. The third pope, Sixtus II, supported the theological position of his predecessor but tolerated the diversity of theological viewpoints and reconciled himself with Cyprian. Both Sixtus and Cyprian were beheaded by Roman authorities within a five-week span in 258.

Institutionalization of the Church in Africa (fourth and early fifth centuries) ‡ The Edict of Milan decreed in 312 that Christianity, along with other religions, was no longer to be persecuted but was to be tolerated. Not until 395 did Christianity become the official state religion of the Roman Empire. This newfound freedom of religious expression had the effect of shifting popular spirituality from martyrdom to monasticism. And the continuing development of the Church's theology led to an ever-increasing precision in the Church's statements of its beliefs.

When everybody was nominally Christian, only a portion were practicing Christians. Many of those who wished to live their faith passionately in the more tolerant age thought that they had to leave the lukewarm waters of the churches in the cities. Thousands, therefore, abandoned the urban centers in favor of the remote deserts.

Finally, in 305, Antony organized monks into worshiping communities who gathered on Saturdays and Sundays, while returning to their individual hermitages the rest of the week. This organization is regarded as the earliest expression of Christian monasticism. Pachomius (c. 292-348) gave full growth to the idea by having monks live, work, and pray together in permanent communities. This movement spread from Upper Egypt to Lower Egypt. Ammon (d.c. 356) created monasteries in about 330 in the Nitrian mountains about seventy miles southeast of his native Alexandria; Macarius (d.c. 390) began monasteries about 330 in the desert at Skete, located along the northwestern border of the Nitrian desert. Thousands of men and women joined these monasteries. At any one time at least three thousand followed Antony and seven thousand followed Pachomius.

After Sts. Clement of Alexandria and Cyprian of Carthage had strengthened the foundation of the Church in the third century, other Fathers of the Church — including Sts. Athanasius, Cyril, Isidore, and Macarius in Egypt; and Augustine and Optatus at Carthage — in the fourth and fifth centuries provided further inspiration and insight for the Church. Also, unsainted scholars like Origen at Alexandria and Tertullian at Carthage are included, according to some sources, among the official list of Fathers of the Church. Ten Africans *in toto* are counted among the Church's eighty-seven Fathers, while three Africans, namely Athanasius, Augustine, and Cyril, are included among the Church's thirty-three Doctors.

The Church in Africa, like the Church universal, became occupied in explaining and defending the Church's teachings against the continuous threats of new heresies, namely Arianism, Donatism, Montanism, and Monophysitism. These heresies focused especially on understanding not only the relation between the divine and human elements in Jesus and the implications for understanding Mary's role as Mother of Jesus but also the Eucharist and the relative authority of the pope at Rome in relation to other bishops.

While the Church's first four ecumenical councils, from the Council of Nicaea in 325 to the Council of Chalcedon in 451, took place in Asia Minor (now Turkey), it is noteworthy that Africans played a central role in these councils, especially Cyril of Alexandria at Ephesus and Dioscorus of Alexandria at Chalcedon. During the same period, numerous local and regional councils were held in northern Africa.

Almost halfway through the fourth century, the Church conducted its first evangelization efforts into Ethiopia. St. Frumentius, a Christian originally from Tyre, had arrived in Ethiopia decades before and held positions of secretary and treasurer in the court of King Ella Amida before becoming the regent for King Azana.[18] When Azana came of age, Frumentius was released from his responsibilities and, on his trip home, visited at Alexandria. Frumentius suggested to Patriarch Athanasius of Alexandria that missionaries be sent to Ethiopia. Athanasius responded that he believed Frumentius would be the ideal missionary. The patriarch ordained the former court official and missioned him to Ethiopia as its first bishop. Significantly, foreign clergy and a foreign mother Church continued to dominate the Ethiopian Church from its origin until the twentieth century.

Barbarian Invasion and Occupation (429-534) ‡ During the century in which the six Germanic-speaking Vandal kings ruled in North Africa, the Church flourished in its desert monasteries but suffered significant persecution in its urban centers.

All of the Vandal kings held to the Arian heresy. They generally aimed to eliminate from North Africa the Christian bishops and to replace them with Arian bishops. The first two kings almost succeeded. In Carthage alone, under Genseric (428-477) the number of Catholic bishops was reduced from one hundred sixty-four to three.[19] Genseric's son Huneric (477-484) took up where the father had left off. The new king ordered all the Catholic bishops remaining in northern Africa to come to Carthage in 484 under the pretext of holding theological discussions with the Arians. Once they were there, however, the king exiled the religious leaders either to Corsica or the surrounding desert. The brutal Huneric scourged and exiled five hundred clerics, five thousand laity, and, in an attempt to extirpate the monastic life, ordered all monks and monasteries to be handed over to the dreaded Mauri. When Huneric died, a respite followed with the reign of Gunthamund (484-496), who allowed all the exiled bishops to return home. The worst was yet to come, however. It arrived in the person of Thrasimund (496-523). He prohibited the election of any new bishop. When the province of Byzacena resisted, the king exiled one hundred twenty bishops to Sardinia.

> But who could describe in fitting language or confine himself to just a brief account of the different punishments which the Vandals, on the order of the king, inflicted on their own people? If a writer tried to recount the things which were done in Carthage itself one by one, without any ornament of speech, he would not even be able to indicate the names of the torments. The evidence can easily be viewed today. You can look upon people without hands, others without eyes, others who have no feet, others whose noses and ears have been cut off; and you can see others, left hanging for too long a period, whose heads, which used to be held normally, have been plunged between their shoulders, and who

have protruding shoulder blades. This occurred because they [the king's soldiers] tortured some by hanging them from high buildings and swinging them to and fro through the empty air by jerking ropes with their hands. In some cases the ropes broke, and those who had been hung so high fell down with great force. Many of these people lost skulls, together with their eyes; others died immediately, their bones broken; while others expired shortly afterwards.[20]

Thrasimund's successor, Hilderic (523-530), recalled the exiles. The last king, Gelmer (530-534), soon was defeated militarily by General Belisarius acting on behalf of Emperor Justinian I, the head of the Roman Empire at Constantinople. Political antipathies between Africa and the imperial powers at Constantinople evolved into a political vacuum. "The sixth-century Byzantine failure to reunite the Roman world was final. From then on, the Christian world was to be divided, and Islam was to emerge from Arabia in the middle of the seventh century as a third heir to the Hellenic synthesis."[21]

II. The second seven hundred years: the Islamic expansion and near elimination of the Catholic Church in North Africa.

What began in the middle of the seventh century as a military victory ended half a century later as a religious and cultural victory. "In 642, only ten years after the death of Muhammad, Alexandria was surrendered to the Islamic Arab army, and the province of Egypt, which for centuries had been one of the most important parts of the Roman-Byzantine Empire and of the Christian Church, became from then on a central pillar of Islam."[22]

The most striking of all effects produced by the Arab conquest of North Africa was the gradual but almost complete disappearance of Christianity. The Berbers not only accepted Mohammedanism, they became its most fanatical defenders. Doubtless economic considerations entered: non-Muslims paid a head tax, and converts were for a time freed from it. When in 744, the Arab governor of Egypt offered this exemption, 24,000 Christians went over to Islam. Occasional but severe persecutions of Christians may have influenced many to conform to the ruling faith. In Egypt a Coptic minority held out bravely, built their churches like fortresses, maintained their worship in secret, and survive to this day. But the once crowded churches of Alexandria, Cyrene, Carthage, and Hippo were emptied and decayed; the memory of Athanasius, Cyril, and Augustine faded out; and the disputes of Arians, Donatists, and Monophysites gave way to the quarrels of Sunni and Ismaili Mohammedanism.[23]

With a foothold in Egypt, the politico-military caliphs of Islam extended their hegemony over all of North Africa. During the next fifty years, eight campaigns were launched in order to subdue resistance by the Christian Berbers. The end came when Carthage fell in 694. Christianity was revived momentarily by a Byzantine recovery in 695, but the north breathed its last corporate gasp in 698. Catholic Christian North Africa was left to become a shadow of its former self. During the half-century of wars, many Christians had fled across the Mediterranean to Italy, Sicily, and Spain; those who remained succumbed to the active discrimination by a war-calloused people. "New churches could never be built, the public expression of religion was almost always prohibited. Everywhere such a condition has tended over the generations to the annihilation of minorities."[24]

It is one of the more curious facts of African history that Christianity has survived vigorously for many hundreds of years in Egypt. What differences existed between this land and North Africa? One scholar observes, "The strength of the Coptic Church lay in the combination of monasteries, many of them in rather remote places, and a numerous married clergy." The Church had extended itself geographically beyond the population centers of the Nile's delta and riverbanks to the surrounding deserts and had rooted itself among common people socially through the priests of the Coptic rite, who were not bound to celibacy like priests of the Roman rite. The numerous desert monasteries provided continuing public legitimacy by their reputations for sanctity, scholarship, and wisdom.

Politically, the Egyptians were accustomed to foreign rule. They had been occupied by the Persians in 525 B.C. under Cambyses and again, after local reassertion, by Artaxerxes III in 343; by the Greeks ever since the time of Alexander in 332 B.C.; and by the Romans under Octavian in 30 B.C. When the Arabians arrived in 640, the Egyptians received these invaders as one more foreign power.

As a religious phenomenon, Islam was regarded by many, including St. John Cassian (c. 360-c. 433), as another Christian heresy, similar to the troubling but temporary challenges of Arianism and Donatism. Even successive dynasties of caliphs tolerated Christians, although in ever-lessening degrees: the Fatimids (967-1171) were quite tolerant, with the notable exception of al-Hakim; the Ayyudid dynasty (1171-1250) was less tolerant; and the Mameluke rule (1250-1517) was least so. In this last dynasty, the Church dropped Coptic as its traditional language and, except for liturgies, adopted Arabic. It also changed its episcopal see from Alexandria to Cairo. The Church yielded to the new realities of the de-Christianized context in which it struggled to survive. Oppression continued to be waged by the majority against the minority, as demonstrated in 1320, when fifty-four churches were destroyed. When finally the Mameluke

Empire lost power, the vacuum was filled by the Ottomans at Constantinople. At that time, the Church at Rome had an opportunity to reestablish its influence, when the Copts and the Roman Church entered into a short-lived union. Rome, however, had little interest in maintaining the union; and the Copts risked their very survival by allying themselves with a foreign religion and political power. "From the fifteenth to the eighteenth century the Coptic Church went through a long dark tunnel about which we know rather little. Yet it survived."[26]

South of Upper Egypt, at the confluence of the Blue Nile and White Nile rivers in the Sudan, lay the ancient kingdom of Nubia, which once boasted of a thriving Christianity. Over the course of many centuries, however, the Christian religion lost its vitality and evaporated totally, although imperceptibly. As early as the late fourth century and probably sooner, Christianity had taken root here. The religion prospered here in the seventh century at the same time that Christianity lost its prominence in Egypt. The Nubians had resisted the Islamic advance and, in 652, signed a treaty whereby the Nubians agreed to pay an annual tribute of slaves to the Muslim leaders at Egypt. The Muslims agreed that no Muslim would ever enter the country. From the eighth to the twelfth centuries, Christian Nubia enjoyed a golden era. In the midst of these centuries, "Christianity in Nubia could be ranked among the healthiest on earth."[27] Cathedrals and monasteries were built and decorated magnificently. Numerous native bishops, who had been ordained by the patriarch of Alexandria, filled the local sees. The Nubian vernacular became the ecclesiastical language used in communicating legal documents and recording the lives of the saints.

In the next few centuries, however, a political change affected the Christian country's religious roots. This development began in the thirteenth century, when a Muslim took over as ruler in Nubia's northern kingdom. The kingdom's central authority had lost its vitality. Disparate local fiefdoms sprang up. The southern kingdom too succumbed to this political disorganization. The hierarchical Church had depended on a strong monarchical political government. "Without a strong and supportive monarchy the Church too declined."[28]

Christianity in Nubia maintained itself for many more centuries, but only as a shadow of its former strength. A breakaway kingdom in the north preserved the faith and religion up to the end of the fifteenth century. An isolated island community kept the faith into the middle of the eighteenth century. The die, however, had been cast. In the 1520s, a traveler tells of "150 churches still containing crucifixes and paintings of Our Lady. The people of this country . . . were now neither Christians, Muslims, nor Jews, yet still 'lived in the desire of being Christians.' "[29] This same visitor reported that while he was visiting Ethiopia, six Nubians requested of the Ethiopian emperor that he send priests and monks to Nubia, which was becoming devoid of priests. The emperor reluctantly refused because, as he explained, even Ethiopia's bishop himself had to be sent from Egypt, and he had no priests in Ethiopia to minister to his own people, let alone send priests to Nubia. Christianity in Nubia lacked priests and lacked influence when the monarchical political system evaporated.

Farther south of ancient Nubia lay Ethiopia, which once claimed about one quarter of the territory of Africa. This kingdom evidenced international contacts with the Jewish religion as far back as the Old Testament. Jewish ritualistic circumcision and avoidance of women in menstruation still occur in Ethiopia. The Ethiopian eunuch of Queen Candace was converted by the apostle Philip.[30] He may have brought the new religion to his native land. Another possibility is the popular story that the two youths Frumentius and Aedesius, when they were sailing from Tyre in Syria to India, stopped in Ethiopia for fresh supplies, but pirates captured them. Most of the crew were slaughtered, but the two youths were sent to serve at the court of the king. Decades later, Frumentius was emancipated from the service at the royal court and, while visiting at Alexandria en route to his home, he asked the patriarch to send native clergy to this people, who were very receptive to the Christian religion. The patriarch responded by ordaining and missioning Frumentius himself. So began the long tradition of Alexandria supplying the head of the Church at Ethiopia. The Church survived in Ethiopia because of its geographical isolation by its celibate monks, and sociocultural penetration by its married clergy.

One critic comments, "Thus at times violently but more often quietly enough, did Islam advance while Christianity, like an ill-adapted dinosaur, declined and expired in place after place, crushed essentially by its own limitations, its fossilized traditions, and the lack of a truly viable, self-renewing structure."[31]

III. The last six hundred years: the Christianization of sub-Saharan Africa.

Colonization and Frustration at Evangelization (fifteenth to nineteenth centuries) ‡ The Age of Exploration prepared the way for the Christianization of Africa. The Portuguese led the procession of foreign powers, followed by the Dutch, French, and English. Accompanying the sailors and governmental administrators were merchants and clergy. Colonization and Christianization went hand in hand. The flag of a European country and the cross of Christianity were planted side by side on the African coast from Morocco, westward to the Azores and Cape Verde Islands, southward to the Cape of Good Hope, and northward up to Madagascar and Ethiopia. Catholic dioceses were established at Tangier (1468), Safi (1487), Ethiopia (1555), Cape Verde (1533), and San Salvador (1597). Missionaries began evangelization programs at Ceuta (1415), Benin (1485),

Congo (1490), Angola (1550), Monomotapa (c. 1560), Mozambique (1577), and Sofala (1581). The first native sub-Saharan bishop, Don Henrique of the Congo, was ordained in 1518. Pope Gregroy XV created in 1622 the Congregation of the Faith to organize and expand the Church's missionary movement in Africa.

Men's religious orders and secular clergy from colonial countries generously gave of their personnel and finances to increase gradually the Church's presence by establishing parishes, then dioceses, schools, and finally seminaries. In the 1400s and 1500s, Augustinians, Carmelites and Discalced Carmelites, Dominicans, Franciscans, and Jesuits spread the word of God in Africa. In the 1600s and 1700s, the Brothers of St. John of God, Capuchins, Franciscans Regular Tertiaries, the Holy Ghost Fathers, and the Vincentians entered the Church's mission in sub-Saharan Africa. The missionary movements of these four hundred years always began with great inspiration and enthusiasm, but ended virtually always in failure after a few years or decades of apparent success. Internally, the movement suffered the ill effects of disease, diet, persecution, expulsion, murder, tribal wars, and religious resistance from pagans and Muslims. Many missionaries ended up ministering in coastal cities almost entirely to resident and transient Europeans. Externally, the lifeline of personnel grew quite costly and almost collapsed because of the suppression of the Jesuits in Portugal, the loss of Church personnel and Church status after the French Revolution, and the cultural impact of the Age of Enlightenment, which promoted the valuation of reason over faith. When the colonial political powers attacked each other in territorial wars, the victors refused to send the clergy needed to support the defeated country's ecclesiastical mission. After the Reformation, Protestants and Catholics strove to impede each other's Church work, even within the same country's colony. In a larger context, colonization cast a pall over Christianization because of countries' dominant interest in political and economic benefit rather than religious purpose.

What remained of the Church's efforts from 180 to 1800 for the Christianization of Africa? "After the exuberant flowering of the early Christian centuries in Egypt and Roman Africa, and the later attempts during the seventeenth and eighteenth centuries following the Portuguese discoveries, Christianity almost completely disappeared from the African continent by the beginning of the nineteenth century. Everything had to begin anew."[32]

Missionary Revival (nineteenth to mid–twentieth centuries) ‡

In 1830, when France won military control over Algeria, "many in Europe hailed the event as the harbinger of a new era of Catholicity in Africa."[33] For almost forty years, however, French authorities prohibited Bishops Dupuch and Pavy of Algiers not only from evangelizing the Muslim population but even from hanging crucifixes in Catholic hospitals. The dream of restoring Christianity took on a new excitement in 1849, however, when the Protestant missionary David Livingstone penetrated the interior of sub-Saharan Africa and successfully evangelized the local tribes. Hope for a Christian Africa was reborn.

Another breakthrough occurred in 1867, when Charles Martial Allemand Lavigerie, the Catholic bishop of Nancy in France, was appointed archbishop of Algiers. Ignoring the limitations imposed by the French and their seductive offer of a principal diocese for him in France if he were to abandon his ministry in Africa, he committed himself wholeheartedly to the evangelization of the continent in the southern hemisphere. He founded the Society of Missionaries of Africa, who became known popularly as the White Fathers because of the color of their cassocks. Archbishop Lavigerie and others like him discovered, however, that they could not crack the Muslim strong-hold on North Africa. In half a century from 1873 to 1927, fewer than one thousand conversions were made.[34]

Lavigerie, following the dream envisioned by Livingstone, missioned his priests to equatorial Uganda. In 1879, the arch-bishop began, against great odds of climate, culture, health, and safety, the great Catholic evangelization of sub-Saharan Africa. Swift and extensive progress was made. Other religious com-munities joined Lavigerie. By the end of the century, the mis-sionary communities leading the evangelization of Africa included the Capuchins, Holy Ghost Fathers, Jesuits, Marianhill Fathers, Oblates of Mary Immaculate, Scheut Fathers, Society of African Missions, Trappist monks, Verona Fathers, Vincentian Fathers and Brothers, and White Fathers.[35]

Colonization and Christianization fit together like hand and glove. The mother country supplied clergy for her colo-nies. The Belgian Congo was manned by Belgian missionar-ies while Italians served in Ethiopia and Somaliland. French West Africa, North Africa, Equatorial Africa, Senegal, and Madagascar were reserved for the French clergy. South Africa, Rhodesia, Gambia, Nigeria, Gold Coast, Uganda, Sudan, Egypt, British East Africa, and British Congo became the domain of Great Britain. The Portuguese ministered at Portuguese West Africa and Mozambique. Germany missioned their compa-triots to German Southwest Africa, German East Africa, and Cameroon. Prior to European colonization, the political map of sub-Saharan Africa consisted of countless tribal lands, but between 1870 and the end of the World War I, the colonial powers carved up and parceled out the continent. While evan-gelization was not a primary intention of the European colo-nization, conversion to the religion of the mother country nonetheless occurred and supported the overall vision of the parent country.

Thus it is clear that the Catholic Church has become present everywhere in Africa, and that this presence is the result of only one century of apostolate. The 50,000 Catholics in 1800 increased to 26 million by 1961. In 1800 ecclesiastical divisions were rare; in 1964 there were 312 dioceses, vicariates, or prefectures. . . . The 50 missionaries of 1800 increased to 13,500 priests (2,500 Africans), 5,000 teaching brothers (1,200 Africans), 23,000 religious women (7,000 Africans), and more than 100,000 African catechists or teachers. . . . In a total population of 230 million in 1964, Christians numbered 50 million (26 million Catholics, 19 million Protestants, 5 million Orthodox); Muslims, 95 million; pagans, 85 million. Catholics represented about 12 per cent of the population.[36]

The method of missionizing had shifted with the changes in colonization. Transportation made possible the travel from the capital city into the surrounding countryside. Social development required expansion from the parish church into schools, hospitals, and orphanages.

Independent and Christian Africa (1960 to the present) ✝ The year 1960 is referred to as "the year of African Independence." In that year, eighteen nations declared freedom from European colonial powers.[37] Between 1961 and 1964, another nine nations claimed independence.[38] In 1990, the last colonial territory in Africa achieved statehood and called itself Namibia. Today, fifty-five African nations enjoy political independence.

Between 1963 and 1965, the Roman Catholic Church conducted its twenty-first ecumenical council, namely Vatican Council II. The council's originating spirit, *aggiornamento*, meant, as Pope Paul said during the final session, "From now on *aggiornamento* will signify for us a wisely undertaken quest for a deeper understanding of the spirit of the Council and the faithful application of the norms it has happily and prayerfully pro-vided."[39] The council's *Decree on the Church's Missionary Activity*, *Declaration on the Relationship of the Church to Non-Christian Re-ligions*, and the *Declaration on Religious Freedom* dealt with the Church's missionary efforts worldwide and respect for each person's religious conscience.

The council's consequences are making much impact on Africa. Catholicism and Christianity continue to grow rapidly; approximately fifteen thousand new Christians are added daily to the roles of the Christian churches. Young men and women join the ranks of the Catholic clergy and nuns at very high rates; nonetheless, many regions remain without clergy because the local population burgeons at rates higher than religious vo-cations. The Church in Africa is developing its own identity; it resists Western customs that fail to respect African traditions. None other than Cardinal Malula of Zaire challenges non-Af-ricans who attempt to impose Western ways on African culture: "We deny anyone the right to say, in our place, what are the problems we encounter in our faith."[40] Because Vatican II has instructed Catholics to value other religions, a temporary mis-sionary moratorium resulted, whereby foreign clergy rethought why and how they would evangelize in a land that abounds with native religions and why Western men and women would leave their secularized post-Christian civilization to evangelize abroad rather than at home.

Regarding respect for popular religion and indigenous ex-pressions of religion, tensions have arisen between theory and practice. "The 'de-mystification' of folk Catholicism left many troubled and alienated. It was precisely such elements as heal-ing shrines, protective scapulars, statues, candles, and holy water that were closest to traditionalist religion."[41] Critics "have warned of a 'tyranny of good taste,' whereby Catholic intellectuals have removed loved statues because they are bad art, and popular devotions because they are of relatively recent origin."[42] Despite Vatican II's attempted decentralization of the role of the Blessed Virgin Mary, or perhaps because of this reorientation, alleged appearances of Mary have proliferated worldwide and in Africa as well, specifically in Egypt, Rwanda, Cameroon, and Kenya.

In 1994, Pope John Paul II convened the month-long Synod of Africa. A Pan-African assembly had been desired ever since the conclusion of Vatican II, which had focused mostly on developments within the Euro-centric Church. Africans wanted to discuss issues especially relevant to Africans. The pope suggested a structure that assured the success of the synod. He appointed as *ex officio* members of the synod the two dozen leaders of the Vatican offices, thereby requiring these officials to attend all the synod sessions and to hear what the African bishops were saying. The pope too attended the sessions until an injury prevented him from attending further. Contrary to the original expectation of the African bishops, the pope insisted that the synod be held at Rome; "this 'disaster' turned out to be a blessing in disguise."[43] Bishops came and stayed for all the sessions: of the continent's four hundred forty dioceses, two hundred twenty were represented by their ordinaries. The synod discussions and teachings provided great fruit.

> The bishops came home from the Synod with the good news: they had found a new image of the Church, which is corresponding well to African culture and on which one could hinge the whole of African Church life, namely *the Church as family,* the Family of God in Africa. Indeed, this Church model is full of implications: starting with the bishop (no more "his lordship" but an understanding and compassionate father); the laity (no more inferior helpers of the clergy, but sharing an equal responsibility

as adult family members with their elder brothers, the priests) — the whole Church a "home," giving a sense of belonging, since it is a community "from which absolutely nobody is excluded," and with a welcome access to the family meal, the holy Eucharist. Moreover, this African Church is an extended family with a diversity of tasks and ministries, ruled by the principles of solidarity and subsidiarity and kept working by dialogue: dialogue with its own members and with other churches and religions.[44]

The issues that the bishops discussed in their sixty-four propositions concerned evangelization, inculturation, dialogue with traditional religions, Christian brethren and Muslims, pastoral care in social areas (including the various crises stemming from the AIDS epidemic), and the challenges presented by modern means of social communication. The central theme of Church-as-family was agreed to be a most appropriate symbol for Africans and the Church. The critical issue of marriage, however, was not discussed directly. "The most vital subject of marriage was eliminated under the pretext that the question had already been treated in the general Synod of 1980."[45] It was envisioned that at the completion of the synod, study groups would be commissioned on the vital topics of marriage, ancestors, and the spirit world.

Pope John Paul II delivered his post-synodal apostolic exhortation *Ecclesia in Africa* at Cameroon in September 1995. In that document, he reviewed the synod's origins, development, and discussions. He outlined the challenges facing the Church in Africa as it approached the Jubilee Year and the millennium. He reminded readers that he had traveled to Africa on ten trips and had visited thirty-six of the fifty-five countries. In reviewing the two-thousand-year history of the Church in Africa, the pope recognized and paid homage to the missionaries of the nineteenth century whose efforts at evangelization were particularly fruitful. He lamented the political turmoil and socioeconomic sufferings of the people of the continent. He highlights evangelization by inculturation.

> Inculturation includes two dimensions: on the one hand, "the intimate transformation of authentic cultural values through their integration in Christianity" and, on the other, "the insertion of Christianity in the various human cultures." The Synod considers inculturation an urgent priority in the life of the particular Churches, for a firm rooting of the Gospel in Africa. It is "a requirement for evangelization," "a path towards full evangelization, and one of the greatest challenges for the Church on the Continent on the eve of the Third Millennium."[46]

The pope wrote that family life is being threatened in Africa. He blamed the United Nations Conference on Family, which was held on African soil at Cairo, in 1994, for mocking the traditional values of African and universal family life. He made a plea to save the family. "Do not allow the International Year of the Family to become the year of the destruction of the family."[47] He called on the clergy, religious, and laity, especially the youth, to witness to the faith in Africa. The kingdom of justice and peace, he pointed out, requires the efforts of all people, whom he begs would work in solidarity with each other. The pope concluded by entrusting Africa and its evangelizing mission to Mary, the Star of Evangelization.

As Africa experiences the turn of the millennium, the continent has become a predominately Christian land. Of the continent's 778 million people, 356 million are identified as Christian and 315 million are Muslims.[48] While almost half of the continent's Muslims live in North Africa, which is ninety percent Muslim, almost all the continent's Christians live in sub-Saharan Africa, except for a small percentage who live in Egypt and Sudan. Catholics represent nearly a third of the Christian population.[49]

GLOSSARY

Acacian Schism — Patriarch Acacius of Constantinople (r. 471-489)) co-authored the *Henoticon* (the *Decree of Union*), which accepted the doctrinal teachings of the first three ecumenical councils but not of the fourth, which was held at Chalcedon in 451. When Pope St. Felix III (r. 483-492) responded by excommunicating Acacius in 484, Acacius removed Felix's name from the diptychs at Constantinople. When Acacius' successors requested that Rome recognize their accessions, Felix required that they remove Acacius' name from their diptychs. Neither side gave in, until 519, when five popes later, Pope St. Hormisdas (r. 514-523), with Patriarch John's acceptance, wrote a document requiring the removal of Acacius' name.

Antiochene — At Antioch in Syria, where "the disciples were first called Christians" (Acts of the Apostles 11:26), theologians from the third to the fifth centuries emphasized a literal interpretation of the Bible in opposition to the theologians at Alexandria who emphasized instead the allegorical interpretation of the Scriptures. Members of these schools applied their respective approaches to interpreting and teaching the relation between Jesus' human and divine natures.

Apollinarianism — In his legitimate opposition to the heresy of the Arians, who taught that Jesus was not equal to but subordinate to the Father, Apollinaris (c. 300-c. 390) created another heresy by overemphasizing the divinity of Christ to the detriment of the humanity of Christ. Apollinaris claimed that Jesus had no human soul and instead that the divine Logos supplied the operations of the soul. Ironically, just as his Arian enemies denied Jesus' divinity, Apollinaris in effect denied Jesus' humanity.

Apostate — An apostate is a baptized Christian who abandons faith in Jesus Christ. The apostate may or may not join or create a non-Christian church, for example, Judaism, Islam, or some form of paganism. An apostate is to be distinguished from a heretic who

197

abandons the Catholic Church in order to create a new Christian church.

Archdeacon — In the early centuries of the Church, the deacon whom the bishop selected from all deacons in a diocese to assist the bishop in liturgical and administrative affairs was called the archdeacon. As a diocese grew in members, wealth, and influence, so did the prestige and power of this episcopal appointee.

Arianism —The Alexandrian priest Arius (c. 250-336) taught that God the Father begot the Son in a way that made the Son temporally and substantially inferior to the Father. Subordinate rather than equal to the Father, the Son participated in the Godhead and served as liaison between God and humankind but without being either truly God or truly man, since the Logos substituted for the Son's human soul. The Son was "the most perfect of creatures but still a creature."[1] The Council of Nicaea in 325 condemned this teaching.

Benedictine — Benedict of Nursia created between 530 and 540 a rule for monks that served as a model rule for the next fourteen centuries. The rule provided advice for all ranks of members within the monastic community and rules of conduct that divided the waking day into three relatively equal parts for time spent in prayer, spiritual reading, and manual labor.

Byzantine —The Byzantine Empire originated in A.D. 330, when Emperor Constantine the Great, while maintaining Rome as the imperial capital in the western part of the Roman Empire, moved to Constantinople (now Istanbul in Turkey) and established that site as the capital city in the eastern half of the empire. Theoretically, the two halves were to remain one empire, but when Emperor Theodosius I (r. 379-395) died, the two halves became separate entities. In the West, Rome soon succumbed to, and eventually collapsed under, successive waves of barbarian migrations and assaults on the Eternal City. In the East, Constantinople burgeoned politically, economically, and culturally. The Byzantine Empire lasted over a thousand years, that is, until 1453. The Byzantine Empire became noted for its cooperation, and virtual identification, between the Christian Church and the autocratic state.

The Cells — See *desert monasteries*.

Cenobitical — From the Greek *koinos,* meaning "common," and *bios,* meaning "life," this word describes the communal life of monks in contrast to the solitary life of hermits.

Chilianism — This belief held that Jesus personally and visibly would rule the earth for a thousand years before the end of the world. Before this millennium event would take place, a general resurrection of the just would occur and immediately after its conclusion a general resurrection of the damned would happen.

Council of Chalcedon — Emperor Marcian (r. 450-457) convened this fourth ecumenical council (451) after Pope St. Leo I (r. 440-461) suggested that it was necessary to settle disputes left unresolved from the previous ecumenical council and the Robber Synod, both of which had been held at Ephesus in 431. The council decreed that the Incarnate Word enjoyed a perfect integrity of both divine and human natures. Approximately three hundred fifty bishops attended, almost all of whom came from the East, except three papal legates from Rome and two bishops from Africa.

Council of Constantinople — This second ecumenical council (381) was convoked by Emperor Theodosius I (r. 379-395) and was led by Meletius of Antioch without the presence of Pope St. Damasus I (r. 366-384), since the council had originated as a synod of the Eastern Church rather than an ecumenical council. The council defined the divine nature of the Holy Spirit. In 451, the Council of Chalcedon raised the Council of Constantinople to the status of an ecumenical council.

Council of Ephesus — This third ecumenical council (431) was convoked by Emperor Theodosius II (r. 408-450) and was chaired by St. Cyril of Alexandria (d. 444), who was representing Pope St. Celestine I (r. 422-432). This council defined the divine motherhood of the Blessed Virgin Mary.

Council of Nicaea — Emperor Constantine I (r. 307-337) convened and Pope St. Sylvester I (r. 314-335) conducted this first ecumenical council (325), which defined Jesus' nature as both Son of God and Son of man.

Desert monasteries — The fourth-century *History of the Monks in Egypt* identifies more than a dozen sites where monks lived, worked, and prayed. The region's most important sites were (1) at Colzim, located east of the Nile River and close to the Red Sea, *St. Anthony's monastery;* (2) in the region surrounding Thebes, *the Thebaid,* where Pachomius founded nine monasteries for men and two for women (the most famous of his monasteries was at Tabennisi on the right bank of the Nile); (3) in the Nitrian Valley, on the flat promontory at *Nitria*, located forty miles south of Alexandria, Ammon established a monastic settlement where monks lived in isolation during the week but gathered together on Saturday and Sunday for communal prayer and meals; (4) at Cellia, a dozen miles farther south of Nitria, Ammon founded another monastic settlement called *the Cells*; and (5) at the desert wasteland of *Skete*, about forty miles south of Nitria, Macarius of Alexandria gathered disciples in his monastic system.

Diptychs — The Greek word *diptukon* means "a fold" and is used to describe a two-page writing tablet whose material consisted either of wood, ivory, metal, silver, or gold. Additional pages could be attached as needed. As early as the third century, the Church used these tablets to list the names of martyrs, bishops, and other prominent persons, both living and deceased, who were to be remembered at church services. At first, the lists were read aloud to congregations, but as the lists grew in length, the lists were read quietly by the subdeacon to the presiding bishop or priest. The lists were discontinued in the West by the twelfth century and in the East by the fourteenth century. Conflicts emerged when names of suspected heretics or controversial bishops of one region were removed from the lists of another region.

Donatism — Donatus (d. 347), the bishop of Carthage (r. 313-347), and his numerous disciples taught that sacraments conferred by unworthy priests or bishops were invalid and that recipients of those sacraments needed to receive them again from apparently worthy clerics. Although this schism was condemned by the synods of the Lateran (313), Arles (314), and Milan (316), it spread, nonetheless, across the Roman provinces of Africa. The schism ended when the Vandals in 439 conquered the region and eliminated the schism's proponents.

Eremetical — The Greek word *eremites*, which means "hermit," describes persons who retired from social organization to live in solitude, motivated by the love of God and maintained by the practice of prayer and asceticism. Because of individuals' excesses in asceticism, the Council of Chalcedon (451) required hermits to live under the jurisdiction of abbots or superiors.

Eutychianism — From his monastery on the outskirts of Constantinople the abbot Eutyches (375-454) taught that Jesus' divine nature absorbed his human nature; thereby, in effect, the monk was denying

Jesus' two natures. Numerous disciples further developed this initial error of Eutyches, and these subsequent errors too were attributed to the monk. Ironically, Eutyches was simply trying to oppose Nestorianism and support St. Cyril of Alexandria (d. 444), who taught a subtle formula that the "unlearned, unqualified and imprudent" abbot was unable to grasp with the necessary distinctions.[2] Scholars point out that Eutyches was driven not by malice but by ignorance.

Exegesis — The Greek *exegesis* means "to lead out" and describes the process whereby Scripture scholars explain from the study of words and contexts the fuller meaning of scriptural passages.

Gelasian Sacramentary — This collection of Mass formularies and Mass prayers traditionally has been attributed to Pope St. Gelasius (492-496). Recent scholarship suggests that it seems more historically accurate to hold that the pope created the cultural renaissance that promoted these and other liturgical and theological writings, rather than to suggest that he authored these works.

Gnosticism — This religious philosophy, which teaches that salvation can be achieved by knowledge, has been applied throughout the centuries to many religions. Essentially, gnosticism is a pagan belief that uses the language and images of the religions (Judaism, Christianity, and the Eastern religions), among which it hopes to find acceptance. This approach is used by elites for the elites, the premise being that salvation by revelation is not for everyone but for only those capable of understanding it: "Salvation is accomplished, not by the power of God nor by human faith nor by cooperation with the will of God, but by the assimilation of esoteric knowledge."[3]

Heresy — The Greek *hairesis*, meaning "sect," pertains to truths of faith that are either denied or distorted. Jesus foretold the inevitability of heresy.[4] The early Church witnessed to it.[5] One scholar suggests, "The term 'heresy' has little relevance prior to the fourth century, when ecumenical councils formally defined points of the Faith; for pre-Nicene teaching that deviated from the norm, the term 'heterodoxy' is more appropriate."[6] Teachings traditionally described as heresies prevalent in the early Church in Africa include Arianism, Manichaeanism, Montanism, Nestorianism, and Pelagianism.

Lapsi — The Latin *lapidere* means "to fall" and is applied to describe Christians who worshiped Roman gods by offering them incense to avoid Roman persecution of torture, exile, or death.

Manichaeanism — The Persian priest Manes (d.c. 277) proclaimed himself to be the last great prophet, whose God-given mission was to complete the ethical work begun by Buddha, Zoroaster, and Christ. Manes taught that individuals can break the cosmic cycle of good versus evil, light versus darkness, by entering into themselves and becoming part of the Church of the mind, the Church of the elect. The means to accomplish this struggle consisted of strict asceticism, vegetarianism, and celibacy. Manes's disciples brought this religion to the Roman Empire, including Egypt, around A.D. 300. St. Augustine of Hippo (354-430) followed the Manichaean way for at least nine years before converting to Catholicism. Manichaean missionaries spread this teaching to central and eastern Asia, where it survived until the fourteenth century.

Meletians — Bishop Meletius of Lycopolis at Egypt (d.c. 328) and his disciples condemned, without the possibility of forgiveness, those who had lapsed under the Diocletian persecution.

Monophysitism — The heretical position of Monophysitism, from the Greek *mon*, meaning "one," and *physus*, meaning "nature," was condemned at the Council of Chalcedon (451). Adherents of Monophysitism overemphasized the divine nature of Jesus to the detriment and apparent denial of Jesus' human nature. Ironically, this view had originated in an attempt to avoid Nestorianism, which taught that both the divine and human natures existed and coalesced in Christ. Monophysitism's theological error had its roots in language rather than in concept; "the rejection of the Chalcedonian doctrine was verbal or semantic rather than truly doctrinal."[7] Few Monophysites intended to deny Jesus' humanity.

Montanism — The pagan Montanus (d. 156 or 172) converted to Christianity and soon gathered a group of enthusiasts who claimed special illumination from the Holy Spirit. These spiritual elitists not only lived a strict morality and rigorous austerity but also claimed the charismatic gift of speaking in tongues and proclaimed the imminent end of the world. Despite having been condemned by successive popes almost as soon as the group started, the movement continued in the West until Emperor Honorius (r. 395-423) outlawed it and in the East until Emperor Julian the Apostate (r. 332-363) crushed it. In Africa, Apollinaris of Hierapolis (d.c. 170) was Montanism's most significant opponent.

Nestorianism — Although a firm opponent of Arianism and Pelagianism,

Nestorius (c. 381-451) created his own heresy by calling Mary *Christotokos*, which means "Christ-bearer" or "Mother of Christ," rather than *Theotokos*, which means "God-bearer" or "Mother of God." He taught that Mary was the Mother of Christ but not the Mother of God. Nestorius reasoned that if Mary were to give life to God, then she would have to have been divine. In an attempt to maintain Mary's humanity, Nestorius denied Jesus' divinity.

Nitria — See *desert monasteries*.

Novatianism — Well educated in Latin, philosophy, and theology, Novatian (c. 200-258) was the Church's first author in Latin. While he intended to defend the Church's teaching on the Trinity, his inadequate concepts and language opened the way for what is regarded as heretical developments. "For the most part the fault lies in an insufficient analysis using expressions as yet untroubled by future strife."[8] In 251, when three bishops ordained Novatian bishop in protest against the pope's forgiving attitude toward the lapsed, a synod of sixty bishops excommunicated him on grounds of his rigorist view of sin and narrow approach to conditions for membership in the Church. Novatian's personal appeal and theological skill enabled him to develop schismatic churches in almost all the major cities of the Roman Empire. He suffered martyrdom at Rome under Emperor Valerian (r. 253-260). By the end of the seventh century, Novatianism died out.

Origen — Born, raised, and educated at Alexander by his father, who was martyred by the African-born Roman emperor Septimus Severus (r. 193-211), Origen (c. 184-c. 253), at eighteen, founded a school of grammar, and soon afterward a catechetical school for catechumens at the suggestion of Bishop Demetrius. Wishing to pursue studies in philosophy and the Scriptures in order to dedicate himself to those students more advanced in the faith, Origen turned over to others the care of his schools. Having been forced to flee from Alexandria, when Emperor Caracalla (r. 211-217) initiated an anti-Christian persecution within that city, Origen embarked on a teaching and preaching tour that took him throughout Palestine, Athens, and Rome, then to Cappadocia, Bithynia, and Arabia. After reading Matthew 19:12, Origen castrated himself. Although two councils called by his local bishop criticized Origen for his self-mutilation and for preaching and being ordained without his local bishop's permission, it must be noted that Origen called back others to orthodoxy and died from tortures sustained during the persecution of Emperor Decius (r. 249-251). Some sources include him in the Church's list of Fathers of the Church.[9]

Pelagianism — The monk Pelagius (c. 354-c. 418) left his native Britain, traveled to Rome around 380, and thirty years later moved to Africa, where he remained for the next eight years until he suddenly disappeared from history. This austere spiritual director taught that human will is completely free without any limitations resulting from original sin. Supposedly, each person is able to achieve his or her own moral good, and that nobody needs God's grace to respond to God's commands. Pelagius and his disciples denied both original sin and humankind's inclination to evil.

Platonism — Named for the pre-Christian Athenian philosopher Plato (c. 427-c. 347) and his numerous disciples, this school of thought taught the preeminence of the "world of ideas" and of the spiritual soul, and simultaneously the secondary significance of the material world. This philosophical approach is contrasted often with Aristotelianism, which is named after Plato's student Aristotle (384-322), who emphasized the material world as the fundamental reality.

Rebaptism controversy — St. Cyprian of Carthage (c. 200-258) and Pope St. Stephen (d. 257) took opposing sides in considering whether baptisms were valid when conducted by heretics. Cyprian insisted that the person performing the baptism had to be in union with the Church in order for the baptism to be valid. Stephen taught that it was the Spirit who made the sacrament of baptism effective and valid, and not the agent who performed the baptism.

Robber Synod — See *Synod of the Oak.*

Schism — The Greek word *skhisma,* meaning "separation," describes a breach in a Christian individual or group's full communion with the Church. Schisms, which typically pertain to disciplinary rather than doctrinal matters, are maintained usually by moral rigorists or elitists who refuse either to submit to papal authority or to live in communion with other members of the Church while maintaining orthodox beliefs. "St. Jerome held that schism, begun as an orthodox breach of communion, is so unstable that it will, if continued, wind up in heresy."[10] Schismatics in the early Church in Africa include the Donatists and Novatianists.

Skete — See *desert monasteries.*

Stoicism — This philosophical school was founded by Zeno of Citium in Athens in the fourth century B.C. and influenced many early Church writers, including in Africa both Clement of Alexandria and Tertullian. Stoicism focused on the seriousness of life rather than life's joys, individual needs rather than universal similarities among people, immediate and material concerns rather than transcendent and abstract ideas. Stoics taught the importance of God's existence, the human soul, and ethical behavior; but they understood the divine and human as basically material, not spiritual, and ethics as an independent indifferentism rather than as an interdependent expression of Christian love.

Sub-Sahara — The world's largest desert, specifically the Sahara Desert, divides the world's second largest continent, namely Africa, into two geopolitical regions: North Africa and sub-Saharan Africa.

Synod of the Oak — Theophilus, the patriarch of Alexandria, convened a synod in 403 at a suburb of Chalcedon (now in Turkey) called "The Oak" while on his way to a synod convened by Emperor Arcadius (r. 395-408) at Constantinople (now Istanbul). Because Chalcedon was outside the jurisdiction of Theophilus, his synod there was illegal. The thirty-six members of the synod consisted of twenty-nine Egyptian bishops who served under Theophilus's authority and some Ephesian bishops whom John Chrysostom (c. 347-407) had deposed for buying and selling bishoprics. John refused to attend despite three summonses, the first from some of Theophilus's Egyptian bishops, the second from some of his own priests, and the third from the emperor himself. John held his ground. The illegal synod proceeded to find him guilty of forty-six charges. "All charges were frivolous, exaggerated, or totally false."[11]

Tertullian — Born at Carthage, Tertullian (c. 160-220) converted from paganism to Christianity around 195 and became one of the Church's most ardent and eloquent apologists. So successfully did he support asceticism that some opponents identified him with the Montanists, though technically Tertullian never abandoned the orthodoxy of the Church. He is included in some sources among the Church's list of Fathers of the Church.[12]

Thebaid — See *desert monasteries.*

Theotokos — The Greek word *theotokos* means "God-bearer" or "Mother of God." This term was applied to the Blessed Virgin Mary by the Church at the Council of Ephesus (431). The term is based on the theological concept that Mary bore Jesus, who is at one and the same time God and man, possessing both a divine and human nature. Opponents of the term *Theotokos* preferred to speak of Mary as *Christotokos*, which means "Christ-bearer" or "Mother of Christ." They held that Mary gave birth to the man Jesus, that is, to his human nature but not to his divine nature. The Church wanted to maintain clearly that the Word of God was not *in* man, but the Word of God *is* man. In the real world, Jesus is the God-Man, that is, the *Logos*, or the Word of God made flesh who suffered, died, and rose for humankind. Jesus is not just an exemplary man inspired by God but the God-Man himself who naturally identified with both God and man.

Traditores — The Latin *tradere*, which means "to hand over," describes Christians who surrendered to imperial authorities either the Church's sacred texts, vessels, or vestments. The word "traitor" has its root in *tradere*.

Vandals — This barbarian tribe migrated around the year 170 across the Danube River from present-day Hungary to what is now southern Germany and Switzerland, and again moved successfully against the former inhabitants of Gaul in 406 and Spain in 409. Leaving Gibraltar, the Vandals entered North Africa near Tingis, Mauretania (now Morocco), in 429, then swept swiftly on land along the Mediterranean coast after which they conquered Carthage in 439. From that strategic point, these barbarians invaded Sicily, Corsica, and finally Rome in 455. Their power and presence, however, was short-lived; the imperial navy and armored cavalry from Byzantium defeated the Vandals in 535, after which this tribe vanished as a political entity.

INDEX OF SAINTS AND FEAST DAYS

Isidore Bakanja, Bl., August 15

Isidore of Chios, St., May 15

Isidore of Pelusium, St., February 4

James, St. — *see* Marianus

John of Egypt, St., March 27

Josephine Bakhita, St., February 8

Julia of Carthage and Corsica, St., May 22

Macarius the Elder, St., January 15

Macarius the Younger, St., January 2

Majoricus, St. — *see* Dionysia

Marcellinus of Carthage, St., April 6

Marcellinus, St. (with St. Vincent and St. Domninus), April 20

Marcellus, St., October 30

Marianus, St. (with St. James and Companions), April 30

Martin de Porres, St., November 3

Martyrs of the Alexandrian Plague, February 28

Martyrs of Utica, August 24

Mary of Egypt, St., April 2

Maura, St. — *see* Timothy

Maurice, St. (and the Theban Legion), September 22

Maximilian, St., March 12

Melchiades, Pope St., December 10

Monica, St., August 27

Moses the Black, St., August 28

Nemesian, St. (and Companions), September 10

Onuphrius, St., June 12

Optatus, St., June 4

Orsiesius, St., June 15

Pachomius, St., May 9

Pambo, St., July 18

Pantaenus, St., July 7

Paphnutius, St., September 11

Paul the Hermit, St., January 15

Perpetua, St. (with St. Felicity and Companions), March 7

Peter of Alexandria, St., November 26

Pierius, St., November 4

Pierre Toussaint, Ven., June 30

Poemen, St., August 27

Sarmata, St., October 11

Saturninus, St. (with St. Dativus, St. Victoria, and Companions), February 11

Saturus, St. — *see* Armogastes

Shenute, St., July 1

Sazan, St. — *see* Aizan

Speratus, St. (and Companions), July 17

Thais, St., October 8

Theodore the Sanctified, St., April 27

Timothy, St. (with St. Maura), May 3

Victor, Pope St., July 28

Victoria, St. — *see* Saturninus

Victoria Rasomanarivo, Bl., August 21

Vincent, St. — *see* Marcellinus

Zeno of Verona, St., April 12

BIBLIOGRAPHY

The Acts of the Christian Martyrs. Tr. by Herbert Musurillo. Oxford: The Clarendon Press, 1972.

African Synod: Documents, Reflections, Perspectives. Compiled and edited by the Africa Faith and Justice Network under the direction of Maura Browne. Maryknoll, N.Y.: Orbis Books, 1996.

Attwater, Donald. *Martyrs from St. Stephen to John Tung*. New York: Sheed and Ward, 1957.

Augustine (bishop of Hippo). *The Confessions of St. Augustine*. New York: Doubleday Image Book, 1960.

Athanasius. *The Life of Antony*. Tr. by Robert Gregg. New York: Paulist Press, 1980.

Baeteman, J. *A Martyr of Abyssinia: Abba Ghebre Michael, Priest of the Mission*. Emmitsburg, Md.: St. Joseph's, n.d.

Ball, Ann. *Modern Saints: Their Lives and Faces*. Rockford, Ill.: Tan Books and Publishers, Inc., 1983.

_____. *Modern Saints: Their Lives and Faces*. Book Two. Rockford, Ill.: Tan Books and Publishers. Inc., 1990.

Bane, Martin. *Catholic Pioneers in West Africa*. Dublin: Clonmore and Reynolds Ltd., 1956.

Baur, John. *2000 Years of Christianity in Africa: An African Church History*. Nairobi, Kenya: Pauline Publications Africa, 1994.

Belasco, Milton J. and Hammond, Harold E. *The New Africa: History, Culture, People*. Ed. by Edward Graff. Bronxville, N.Y.: Cambridge Book Co., Inc., 1970.

Bibliotheca Sanctorum. Rome: Istituto Giovanni XXIII Della Pontificia Universita Lateranense, 1968.

Boer, Harry R. *A Short History of the Early Church*. Grand Rapids, Mich.: William B. Eerdmans Publishing Co., 1976.

The Book of Saints. Benedictine Monks of Ramsgate Abbey, eds. Wilton, Conn.: Morehouse Publishing, 1989.

Bouchard, Abbé M. *The History of St. Monica*. Tr. by Anthony Farley. New York: P. J. Kenedy and Sons, n.d.

Bouchaud, Joseph. "Africa." *New Catholic Encyclopedia.* Vol. 1, pp. 172-186.

Brown, William Eric. *The Catholic Church in South Africa. From its Origins to the Present Day.* Ed. by Michael Derrick. New York: P. J. Kenedy and Sons, 1960.

Bunson, Matthew. *The Pope Encyclopedia: An A to Z of the Holy See.* New York: Crown Trade Paperbacks, 1995.

Bunson, Matthew; Bunson, Margaret; and Bunson, Stephen. *John Paul II's Book of Saints.* Huntington, Ind.: Our Sunday Visitor Publishing Division, 1999.

Burghardt, Walter John. "Cyril of Alexandria, St." *New Catholic Encyclopedia.* Vol. 4, pp. 571-576.

Butler's Lives of the Saints. Ed. by Herbert Thurston and Donald Attwater. Four volumes. Westminster, Md.: Christian Classics, 1990.

Cassarini, Ernesto. *Il Beato Ghebre Michael.* Rome: Casa Della Missione, 1926.

Cavallini, Giuliana. *St. Martin de Porres: Apostle of Charity.* Tr. by Caroline Holland. St. Louis: B. Herder Book Co., 1963.

Chapin, John. "Gelasius I, Pope, St." *New Catholic Encyclopedia.* Vol. 6, pp. 315-316.

Chenu, Bruno; Prudhomme, Claude; Quere, France; and Thomas, Jean-Claude. *The Book of Christian Martyrs.* New York: The Crossroad Publishing Co., 1990.

Congregatio de Causis Sanctorum. *Index ac Status Causarum.* Città del Vaticano, 1999.

Costelloe, Martin Joseph. "Catherine of Alexandria, St." *New Catholic Encyclopedia.* Vol. 3, p. 253.

Cristiani, Leon. *The Story of Monica and Her Son Augustine.* Tr. by M. Angeline Bouchard. Boston: St. Paul Editions, 1977.

Curtin, Philip and others. *African History.* Boston: Little, Brown and Co., 1964.

Davitt, Thomas. *Justin De Jacobis.* Dublin: The Vincentian Fathers, 1975.

De Murville, M.N.L. Couve. *Slave from Haiti: A Saint for New York? The Life of Pierre Toussaint.* London: Catholic Truth Society, 1995.

Delaney, John J. *Dictionary of Saints*. Garden City, N.Y.: Doubleday and Co., Inc., 1980.

The Documents of Vatican II. Gen. ed., Walter M. Abbott. Tr. ed., Joseph Gallagher. New York: Guild Press, 1966.

Durant, Will. *The Age of Faith: A History of Medieval Civilization — Christian, Islamic, and Judaic — From Constantine to Dante: A.D. 325-1300*. New York: Simon and Schuster, 1950.

Du Roy de Blicquy, Olivier Jean-Baptiste. "Augustine, St." *New Catholic Encyclopedia*. Vol. 1, pp. 1041-1058.

Faupel, John F. *African Holocaust: The Story of the Uganda Martyrs*. New York: P. J. Kenedy, c. 1962.

Frend, W.H.C. *Martyrdom and Persecution in the Early Church: A Study of a Conflict from the Maccabees to Donatus*. Oxford: Basil Blackwell, 1965.

Gavigan, John Joseph. "North Africa, Early Church In." *New Catholic Encyclopedia*. Vol. 10, pp. 502-505.

Grant, Michael. *Atlas of Classical History: From 1700 BC to AD 565*. New York: Oxford University Press, 1994.

Gregory the Great. *St. Gregory the Great: Dialogues*. Tr. by Odo John Zimmerman. *The Fathers of the Church*. Vol. 39. New York: Fathers of the Church, Inc., 1959.

Harkins, Paul William. "Oak, Synod of the." *New Catholic Encyclopedia*. Vol. 10, p. 589.

Hastings, Adrian. *The Church in Africa 1450-1950: The Oxford History of the Christian Church*. Ed. by Henry and Owen Chadwick. Oxford: Clarendon Press, 1994.

———. *A History of African Christianity 1950-75*. African Studies Series. No. 26. Ed. by John Dunn and others. Cambridge: Cambridge University Press, 1979.

Holland, Caroline Celeste. "Porres, Martin De, St." *New Catholic Encyclopedia*. Vol. 11, pp. 595-596.

Holtzclaw, Robert Fulton. *The Saints Go Marching In*. Shaker Heights, Ohio: The Keeble Press, Inc., 1980.

Isichei, Elizabeth. *A History of Christianity in Africa: From Antiquity to the Present*. Grand Rapids, Mich.: William B. Eerdmans Publishing Co., 1995.

John Paul II, Pope. "Post-Synodal Apostolic Exhortation: The Church in Africa." *The African Synod: Documents, Reflections, Perspectives*. Maryknoll, N.Y.: Orbis Books, 1996.

_____. "Litterae Apostolicae: Dei famulae Victoriae Rasoamanarivo Beatorum honores decernuntur." *Acta Apostolicae Sedis* Vol. LXXXIV (June 2, 1992). No. 6, pp. 493-496.

_____. "Litterae Apostolicae: Venerabilis Serva Dei Anuarita Nengapeta Maria Clementina in Beatorum catalogum refertur." *Acta Apostolicae Sedis*. Vol. LXXXIV (December 5, 1992). No. 12, pp. 1112-1115.

_____. "Litterae Apostolicae: Venerabilis Servo Dei Cypriano Michaeli Iwene Tansi Beatorum honores decernuntur." *Acta Apostolicae Sedis*. Vol. XCI (February 5, 1999). No. 2, pp. 161-162.

The Lives of the Desert Fathers. Tr. by Norman Russell. No. 34 of Cistercian Studies series. Kalamazoo, Mich.: Cistercian Publications, 1980.

Johnston, T. *The Church in North Africa*. Dublin: Office of the "Irish Messenger," 1930.

Kearns, J. C. *The Life of Blessed Martin De Porres*. New York: P. J. Kenedy and Sons, 1937.

Kelly, J.N.D. *The Oxford Dictionary of Popes*. New York: Oxford University Press, 1986.

Kelly, Joseph F. *The Concise Dictionary of Early Christianity*. Collegeville, Minn.: The Liturgical Press, 1992.

King, Noel Q. *Christian and Muslim in Africa*. New York: Harper and Row, Publishers, 1971.

Kirchner, Walther. *Western Civilization to 1500*. New York: Barnes and Noble Books, 1960.

Kritzeck, James. "Islam." *New Catholic Encyclopedia*. Vol. 7, pp. 676-684.

Lawlor, Francis X. "Schism." *New Catholic Encyclopedia*. Vol. 12, pp. 1130-1131.

Le Saint, William. "Tertullian." *New Catholic Encyclopedia*. Vol. 13, pp. 1019-1022.

MacRae, George Winsor. "Gnosticism." *New Catholic Encyclopedia*. Vol. 6, pp. 523-528.

Marion, Francis. *New African Saints: The Twenty-two Marytrs of Uganda.* Milan: Ancora Publisher, 1964.

McBrien, Richard P. *Lives of the Popes: The Pontiffs from St. Peter to John Paul II.* San Francisco: Harper Collins Publishers, 1997.

McKenzie, John L. *Dictionary of the Bible.* Milwaukee: The Bruce Publishing Co., 1965.

Murphy, Francis Xavier. "Isidore of Pelusium." *New Catholic Encyclopedia.* Vol. 7, pp. 673-674.

_____. "Monophysitism." *New Catholic Encyclopedia.* Vol. 9, pp. 1064-1065.

_____. "Pierius, St." *New Catholic Encyclopedia.* Vol. 11, p. 349.

O'Brien, Felicity. *Saints in the Making.* Dublin: Veritas Publications, 1988.

Owens, Guillermo. "Eutychianism." *New Catholic Encyclopedia.* Vol. 5, pp. 642-643.

Ruffin, C. Bernard. *The Days of the Martyrs (A history of the persecutions of Christians from apostolic times to the time of Constantine).* Huntington, Ind.: Our Sunday Visitor, Inc., 1985.

Russell, H. *Africa's Twelve Apostles.* Boston: Daughters of St. Paul, 1981.

Ryan, Edmund Granville. "Dionysius of Alexandria." *New Catholic Encyclopedia.* Vol. 4, pp. 876-877.

The Sayings of the Desert Fathers. Tr. by Benedicta Ward. Kalamazoo, Mich.: Cistercian Publications, 1984.

Scarre, Chris. *The Penguin Historical Atlas of Ancient Rome.* New York: Penguin Books, 1995.

Spanneut, Michel. "Clement of Alexandria." *New Catholic Encyclopedia.* Vol. 3, pp. 943-944.

Victor of Vita: History of the Vandal Persecution. Tr. by John Moorhead. Vol. 10 of the series: translated texts for historians. Liverpool: Liverpool University Press, 1992.

Weyer, Hans. "Novatian and Novatianism." *New Catholic Encyclopedia.* Vol. 10, pp. 534-535.

Whittaker, Molly. "Pantaenus, St." *New Catholic Encyclopedia.* Vol. 10, p. 947.

ABOUT THE AUTHOR

Saints of Africa is Vincent J. O'Malley's third book on the saints of the Catholic Church. At the turn of the new millennium, his *Ordinary Suffering of Extraordinary Saints* was published by Our Sunday Visitor. His first book, *Saintly Companions*, was released five years earlier by another publisher.

The author has been a Vincentian priest for twenty-eight years. During this time he has served mostly in higher education. He has preached numerous retreats, always including themes on the lives of the saints.

Father O'Malley believes that *Saints of Africa* represents the first-ever critical compilation of a cross section of saints of African origin and African descent. Among the almost ninety entries in this book are included some of the most famous saints of the early Church — for example, Augustine, Athanasius, Cyprian, Cyril, as well as Perpetua and Felicity. In addition the stories of many of the most recent saints, blesseds, and venerables of African origin and descent can be found in this volume; among them are the inspiring stories of Charles Lwanga, Cyprian Tansi, Josephine Bakhita, Martin de Porres, and Pierre Toussaint.

CHAPTER NOTES

January

1. *Butler's Lives of the Saints*, ed. by Herbert Thurston and Donald Attwater, four volumes (Westminster, Md.: Christian Classics, 1990), vol. I, p. 6.
2. Ibid.
3. Ibid., p. 20.
4. Ibid., p. 70.
5. Ibid., p. 71.
6. Ibid.
7. Ibid., p. 94.
8. Ibid.
9. Ibid.
10. Ibid., p. 95.
11. Ibid., p. 93.
12. Matthew 19:21.
13. Athanasius, *The Life of Antony*, tr. by Robert Gregg (New York: Paulist Press, 1980), pp. 43–44.
14. Butler, vol. I, p.107.
15. Pope John Paul II, "Litterae Apostolicae: Venerabilis Servo Dei Cypriano Michaeli Iwene Tansi Beatorum honores decernunter," in *Acta Apostolicae Sedis*, vol. XCI (February 5, 1999), No. 2, p. 161.

February

1. Francis Xavier Murphy, "Isidore of Pelusium," in *New Catholic Encyclopedia*, vol. 7, p. 673.
2. Anne Ball, *Modern Saints: Their Lives and Faces* (Rockford, Ill.: Tan Books and Publishers, 1990), Book Two, p. 441.
3. *Bakhita: An Inspiring Life* (Rome: Canossian Generalate, n.d.), p. 33.
4. *Butler's Lives of the Saints*, ed. by Herbert Thurston and Donald Attwater, four volumes (Westminster, Md.: Christian Classics, 1990), vol. I, p 286.
5. Ibid., p. 303.

6. Ibid., pp. 436-437.
7. Donald Attwater, *Martyrs from St. Stephen to John Tung* (New York: Sheed and Ward, 1957), pp. 48-49.

March

1. Bruno Chenu, Claude Prudhomme, France Quere, and Jean-Claude Thomas, *The Book of Christian Martyrs* (New York: The Crossroad Publishing Co., 1990), pp. 62-63.
2. Donald Attwater, *Martyrs from St. Stephen to John Tung* (New York: Sheed and Ward, 1957), p. 23.
3. Chenu and others, p. 63.
4. Attwater, pp. 28-29.
5. *Butler's Lives of the Saints*, ed. by Herbert Thurston and Donald Attwater, four volumes (Westminster, Md.: Christian Classics, 1990), vol. I, p. 498.
6. Ibid., p. 571.
7. Ibid., p. 572.
8. Ibid., p. 573.
9. *Victor of Vita: History of the Vandal Persecution*, tr. by John Moorhead (Liverpool, England: Liverpool University Press, 1992), pp. 12-13.
10. Butler, vol. III, p. 691.
11. Ibid., p. 692.
12. Victor of Vita, p. 19.
13. Ibid.
14. Ibid., p. 21.
15. Ibid., p. 22.
16. Luke 14:26.

April

1. *Butler's Lives of the Saints*, ed. by Herbert Thurston and Donald Attwater, four volumes (Westminster, Md.: Christian Classics, 1990), vol. II, pp. 30-31.
2. Ibid., p. 77.
3. Ibid.
4. Ibid., vol. IV, p. 627.
5. Ibid., pp. 627-628.

6. Donald Attwater, *Martyrs from St. Stephen to John Tung* (New York: Sheed and Ward, 1957), p. 45.

7. Ibid., p. 43.

8. Ibid., p. 46.

May

1. John J. Delaney, *Dictionary of Saints* (Garden City, N.Y.: Doubleday and Co., 1980), p. 53.

2. *Butler's Lives of the Saints*, ed. by Herbert Thurston and Donald Attwater, four volumes (Westminster, Md.: Christian Classics, 1990), vol. II, p. 215.

3. Ibid., pp. 259–260.

4. Ibid., p. 259.

5. Ibid., p. 319.

6. Butler, vol. II, p. 367.

June

1. Donald Attwater, *Martyrs from St. Stephen to John Tung* (New York: Sheed and Ward, 1957), p. 198.

2. Ibid., p. 199.

3. Ibid.

4. John F. Faupel, *African Holocaust: The Story of the Uganda Martyrs* (New York: P. J. Kenedy, c. 1962), pp. 207–217.

5. *Butler's Lives of the Saints*, ed. by Herbert Thurston and Donald Attwater, four volumes (Westminster, Md.: Christian Classics, 1990), vol. II, p. 460.

6. John J. Delaney, *Dictionary of Saints* (New York: Doubleday and Co., 1980), p. 381.

7. Butler, vol. II, p. 547.

8. Ibid., p. 564.

9. Walter J. Burghardt, "Cyril of Alexandria, St.," in *New Catholic Encyclopedia*, vol. 4, p. 571.

10. Ibid., p. 573.

11. Ibid., p. 574.

12. M.N.L. Couve de Murville, *Slave from Haiti: A Saint for New York? The Life of Pierre Toussaint* (London: Catholic Truth Society Publications, 1995), p. 6.

July

1. *Butler's Lives of the Saints*, ed. by Herbert Thurston and Donald Attwater, four volumes (Westminster, Md.: Christian Classics, 1990), vol. III, p. 1.
2. Butler, vol. III, p. 13.
3. *Bibliotheca Sanctorum* (Rome: Istittuto Giovanni XXIII Della Pontificia Universita Lateranense, 1968), vol. X, col. 119; John J. Delaney, *Dictionary of Saints* (New York: Doubleday and Co., 1980), p. 444; M. Whittaker, "Pantanus," in *New Catholic Encyclopedia*, vol. 10, p. 947.
4. Butler, vol. III, pp. 32–33.
5. Ibid., p. 89.
6. Ibid., p. 90.
7. Ibid., p. 125.
8. Ibid., pp. 124–125.
9. Donald Attwater, *Martyrs from St. Stephen to John Tung* (New York: Sheed and Ward, 1957), p. 20.
10. Ibid.
11. Butler, vol. III, p. 137.
12. Ibid.
13. Ibid., p. 138.
14. Ibid., p. 153.
15. *Bibliotheca Sanctorum*, vol. II, col. 610.
16. Richard McBrien, *Lives of the Popes: The Pontiffs from St. Peter to John Paul II* (San Francisco: Harper Collins Publishers, 1997), p. 42.

August

1. *Butler's Lives of the Saints*, ed. by Herbert Thurston and Donald Attwater, four volumes (Westminster, Md.: Christian Classics, 1990), vol. III, p. 349.
2. Felicity O'Brien, *Saints in the Making* (Dublin: Veritas Publications, 1988), pp. 62–63.
3. Ibid., p. 68.
4. Ibid., p. 69.
5. Butler, vol. III, p. 392.
6. John 21:11.
7. Leon Cristiani, *The Story of Monica and Her Son Augustine*, tr. by M. Angeline Bouchard (Boston: St. Paul Editioins, 1977), p. 33.

8. Butler, vol. II, p. 227.
9. Augustine of Hippo, *The Confessions of St. Augustine* (New York: Doubleday and Co., 1960), book 9, chapter 11, paragraph 27, p. 223.
10. *The Sayings of the Desert Fathers*, tr. by Benedicta Ward (Kalamazoo, Mich.: Cistercian Publications, 1984), No. 27, p. 171.
11. Ibid., No. 23, p. 170.
12. Ibid., No. 95, p. 180.
13. Ibid., No. 64, p. 175.
14. Delaney, *Dictionary of Saints* (New York: Doubleday and Co., 1980), p. 58.
15. Augustine, *Confessions*, book 6, chapter 3, paragraph 4, p. 137.
16. Ibid., book 8, chapter 12, paragraph 28, p. 201.
17. Ibid., paragraph 29, p. 202.
18. Romans 13:13-14.
19. Olivier Jean-Baptiste Du Roy de Blicquy, "Augustine, St.," in *New Catholic Encyclopedia*, vol. 1, p. 1048.
20. Butler, vol. III, pp. 435-436.
21. *The Sayings of the Desert Fathers*, tr. by Benedicta Ward (Kalamazoo, Mich.: Cistercian Publications, 1975), No. 2, pp. 138-139.
22. Ibid., No. 3, p. 139.
23. Ibid., p. 436.
24. J. Baeteman, *A Martyr of Abyssinia: Abba Ghebre-Michael, Priest of the Mission* (Emmitsburg, Md.: Saint Joseph's, n.d.), pp. 53-54.

September

1. *Butler's Lives of the Saints*, ed. by Herbert Thurston and Donald Attwater, four volumes (Westminster, Md.: Christian Classics, 1990), vol. III, p. 496.
2. Ibid., p. 527.
3. Ibid.
4. Ibid., pp. 538-539.
5. Donald Attwater, *Martyrs from St. Stephen to John Tung* (New York: Sheed and Ward, 1957), p. 39.
6. Ibid., p. 619.

October

1. See 1 Corinthians 7:7-8.
2. Matthew 5:29-30.

3. Gregory the Great, *Dialogues*, in *The Fathers of the Church*, vol. 39, tr. by Odo John Zimmerman (New York: Fathers of the Church, Inc., 1959), book 3, chapter 11, pp. 125-127.

4. *The Sayings of the Desert Fathers*, tr. by Benedicta Ward (Kalamazoo, Mich.: Cistercian Publications, 1975), No. 2, p. 225.

5. Ibid., No. 3, pp. 225-226.

6. Ibid., No. 5, p. 226.

7. *Victor of Vita: History of the Vandal Persecution*, tr. by John Moorhead (Liverpool: Liverpool University Press, 1992), p. 33.

8. Ibid., p. 192.

9. *The Acts of the Christian Martyrs*, tr. by Herbert Musurillo (Oxford: Clarendon Press, 1972), p. 269.

10. Ibid.

11. Ibid., p. 189.

12. Donald Attwater, *Martyrs from St. Stephen to John Tung* (New York: Sheed and Ward, 1957), p. 55.

13. Ibid.

14. Ibid., pp. 55-56.

November

1. *Butler's Lives of the Saints*, ed. by Herbert Thurston and Donald Attwater, four volumes (Westminster, Md.: Christian Classics, 1990), vol. IV, p. 269.

2. Giuliana Cavallini, *St. Martin de Porres: Apostle of Charity*, tr. by Caroline Holland (St. Louis: B. Herder Book Co., 1963), p. 5.

3. Ibid., p. 7.

4. Psalm 84:10b.

5. Caroline Celeste Holland, "Porres, Martin de, St.," in *New Catholic Encyclopedia*, vol. 11, p. 595.

6. Cavallini, p. 9.

7. Holland, p. 595.

8. Cavallini, p. 115.

9. Matthew 5:29-30.

10. Francis Xavier Murphy, "Pierius, St.," in *New Catholic Encyclopedia*, vol. 11, p. 349.

11. Butler, vol. IV, p. 263.

12. Edmund Granville Ryan, "Dionysius of Alexandria, St.," in *New Catholic Encyclopedia*, vol. 4, pp. 876-877.

13. *Liber Pontificalis*, as noted by John Chapin, "Gelasius I, Pope, St.," in *New Catholic Encyclopedia*, vol. 6, p. 315.

14. Matthew Bunson, *The Pope Encyclopedia: An A to Z of the Holy See* (New York: Crown Trade Paperbacks, 1995), p. 149.

15. J.N.D. Kelly, *The Oxford Dictionary of Popes* (New York: Oxford University Press, 1986), p. 49.

16. John Chapin, "Gelasius I, Pope, St.," in *New Catholic Encyclopedia*, vol. 6, p. 316.

17. Ibid.

18. Martin Joseph Costelloe, "Catherine of Alexandria, St.," in *New Catholic Encyclopedia*, vol. 3, p. 253.

19. Butler, vol. IV, p. 423.

20. Ibid., p. 424.

December

1. Pope John Paul II, *Acta Apostolicae Sedis*, vol. LXXXIV (December 5, 1992), No. 12, p. 1113.

2. Matthew Bunson, Margaret Bunson, and Stephen Bunson, *John Paul II's Book of Saints* (Huntington, Ind.: Our Sunday Visitor Publishing Division, 1999), p. 232.

3. Michel Spanneut, "Clement of Alexandria," in *New Catholic Encyclopedia*, vol. 3, pp. 943-944.

4. Ibid., p. 943.

5. *The Acts of the Christian Martyrs*, tr. by Herbert Musurillo (Oxford: Clarendon Press, 1972), p. 303.

6. Ibid., p. 305.

7. Ibid.

8. Ibid., p. 307.

9. Ibid.

10. Ibid.

11. Ibid., pp. 307, 309.

12. *Victor of Vita: History of the Vandal Persecution*, tr. by John Moorhead (Liverpool: Liverpool University Press, 1992), pp. 71-72.

13. Ibid., p. 72.

14. Ibid., pp. 72-73.

15. The sixth-century *Liber Pontificalis*, as noted in *Butler's Lives of the Saints*, ed. by Herbert Thurston and Donald Attwater, four volumes (Westminster, Md.: Christian Classics, 1990), vol. IV, p. 529; and

Matthew Bunson, *The Pope Encyclopedia: An A to Z of the Holy See* (New York: Crown Trade Paperbacks, 1995), p. 241.

16. Richard McBrien, *Lives of the Popes: The Pontiffs from St. Peter to John Paul II* (San Francisco: Harper Collins Publishers, 1997), p. 57.

17. Butler, vol. IV, p. 587.

A Brief History of the Catholic Church in Africa

1. Matthew 2:13.
2. Matthew 2:15; see Hosea 11:1.
3. Acts of the Apostles 2:5, 10.
4. See Matthew 27:32; Mark 15:21; Luke 23:26.
5. See Acts of the Apostles 13:1.
6. See Acts of the Apostles 8:27-39.
7. Acts of the Apostles 18:24-25, 28.
8. Acts of the Apostles 18:26.
9. 1 Corinthians 3:22-23.
10. 1 Corinthians 3:9; see Titus 3:13.
11. See Mark 14:51-52; Acts of the Apostles 12:12 and 12:25—13:13.
12. See Colossians 4:10, Philemon 1:24, and 2 Timothy 4:11.
13. 1 Peter 5:13.
14. John L. McKenzie, "Mark, Gospel of," *Dictionary of the Bible* (Milwaukee: The Bruce Publishing Co., 1965), p. 543.
15. Chris Scarre, *Chronicle of the Roman Emperors* (London: Thames and Hudson Ltd., 1995), p. 170.
16. Ibid., p. 202.
17. William Le Saint, "Tertullian," in *New Catholic Encyclopedia*, p. 1021.
18. Elizabeth Isichei, *A History of Christianity in Africa: From Antiquity to the Present* (Grand Rapids, Mich.: William B. Eerdmans Publishing Co., 1995), pp. 32-33.
19. John Joseph Gavigan, "North Africa, Early Church In," in *New Catholic Encyclopedia*, vol. 10, p. 504.
20. *Victor of Vita: History of the Vandal Persecution*, tr. by John Moorhead (Liverpool: Liverpool University Press, 1992), p. 77.
21. Philip Curtin and others, *African History* (Boston: Little, Brown and Co., n.d.), p. 66.
22. Adrian Hastings, *The Church in Africa 1450-1950: The Oxford History of the Christian Church*, ed. by Henry and Owen Chadwick (Oxford: Clarendon Press, 1994), p. 55.

23. Will Durant, *The Age of Faith: A History of Medieval Civilization —Christian, Islamic, and Judaic — From Constantine to Dante: A.D. 325-1300* (New York: Simon and Schuster, 1950), p. 289.

24. Hastings, p. 65.

25. Ibid.

26. Ibid., p. 67.

27. Noel Q. King, *Christian and Muslim in Africa* (New York: Harper and Row, Publishers, 1971), p. 9.

28. Ibid., p. 68.

29. Ibid., p. 69.

30. See Acts of the Apostles 8:27-38.

31. Ibid., p. 70.

32. Joseph Bouchaud, "Africa," in *New Catholic Encyclopedia*, vol. 1, p. 176.

33. T. Johnston, *The Church in North Africa* (Dublin: Office of the "Irish Messenger," 1930), p. 22.

34. Ibid., p. 27.

35. Hastings, p. 619.

36. Bouchaud, p. 185.

37. Milton Jay Belasco and Harold E. Hammond, ed. by Edward Graff, *The New Africa: History, Culture, People* (Bronxville, N.Y.: Cambridge Book Co., Inc., 1970), pp. 150-151.

38. Ibid., p. 151.

39. Lawrence Cardinal Sheehan, "Introduction," in *The Documents of Vatican II*, ed. by Walter Abbot, tr. by Joseph Gallagher (New York: Guild Press, 1966), p. xviii.

40. Elizabeth Isichei, *A History of Christianity in Africa: From Antiquity to the Present* (Grand Rapids, Mich.: William B. Eerdmans Publishing Co., 1995), p. 328.

41. Ibid., p. 327.

42. Ibid., p. 328.

43. John Baur, *2000 Years of Christianity in Africa: An African Church History* (Nairobi, Kenya: Pauline Publications Africa, 1998), p. 509.

44. Ibid., pp. 510-511.

45. Ibid., p. 509.

46. John Paul II, "Post-synod apostolic exhortation," in *The African Synod*, p. 250.

47. Ibid., p. 259.

48. www.infoplease.com/ipa/A0001484.html:Religious (Population of the World, 1998).

49. Ibid. Among the Christians are 114 million Roman Catholics, 74 million Protestants, 34 million Orthodox, 28 million Anglicans, 75 million "other Christians," and 32 million unaffiliated Christians.

Glossary

1. Joseph F. Kelly, *The Concise Dictionary of Early Christianity* (Collegeville, Minn.: The Liturgical Press, 1992), p. 17.

2. Guillermo Owens, "Eutychianism," in *New Catholic Encyclopedia*, vol. 5, p. 643.

3. G. W. MacRae, "Gnosticism," in *New Catholic Encyclopedia*, vol. 6, p. 526.

4. See Mark 13:6; Matthew 13:24–39.

5. See Acts of the Apostles 20:30; Colossians 2:18.

6. Kelly, p. 74.

7. Francis Xavier Murphy, "Monophysitism," in *New Catholic Encyclopedia*, vol. 9, p. 1065.

8. Hans Weyer, "Novatian and Novatianism," in *New Catholic Encyclopedia*, vol. 10, p. 535.

9. Matthew Bunson, Margaret Bunson, and Stephen Bunson; *Encyclopedia of Saints* (Huntington, Ind.: Our Sunday Visitor, Inc., 1998), p. 684.

10. Francis X. Lawlor, "Schism," in *New Catholic Encyclopedia*, vol. 12, p. 1130.

11. Paul William Lawlor, "Oak, Synod of the," in *New Catholic Encyclopedia*, vol. 10, p. 589.

12. Bunson, p. 685.